Canadian Exporting

FOR

DUMMIES®

1807
WILEY
2007

John Wiley & Sons Canada, Ltd.

Canadian Exporting For Dummies®

Published by
John Wiley & Sons Canada, Ltd.
6045 Freemont Blvd.
Mississauga, ON L5R 4J3
www.wiley.ca

For details on how to create a custom book for your company or organization, or for more information on John Wiley & Sons Canada custom publishing program, please call 416-646-7992 or e-mail us at cupubcan@wiley.com

Canadian Exporting For Dummies

ISBN 13: 978-0-470-84076-4

Printed in Canada

1 2 3 4 5 TRI 11 10 09 08 07

Distributed in Canada by John Wiley & Sons Canada, Ltd.

For general information on John Wiley & Sons Canada, Ltd, including all books published by Wiley Publishing, Inc., please call our warehouse, Tel 1-800-567-4797. For reseller information, including discounts and premium sales, please call our sales department, Tel 416-646-7992. For press review copies, author interviews, or other publicity information, please contact our marketing department, Tel 416-646-4584, Fax 416-236-4448.

Table of Contents

Publisher's Acknowledgements

We're proud of this book; please send us your comments at canadapt@wiley.com. Some of the people who helped bring this book to market include the following:

Acquisitions, Editorial, and Media Development

Editor: Robert Hickey

Developmental Editor: Greg Ioannou, Colborne Communications

Writers: Heather Ball and Stacey Curtis, Colborne Communications

Copy Editor: Rachel Rosen, Colborne Communications

Manager, Custom Publications: Christiane Coté

Project Manager: Liz McCurdy

Project Coordinator: Pamela Vokey

Cartoons: Rich Tennant (www.the5thwave.com)

Wiley Bicentennial Logo: Richard J. Pacifico

Production

Publishing Services Director: Karen Bryan

Publishing Services Manager: Ian Koo

Layout: Pat Loi

Proofreader: Liisa Kelly, Colborne Communications

John Wiley & Sons Canada, Ltd.

Bill Zerter, Chief Operating Officer

Jennifer Smith, Publisher, Professional and Trade Division

Publishing and Editorial for Consumer Dummies

Diane Graves Steele, Vice President and Publisher, Consumer Dummies

Joyce Pepple, Acquisitions Director, Consumer Dummies

Kristin A. Cocks, Product Development Director, Consumer Dummies

Michael Spring, Vice President and Publisher, Travel

Kelly Regan, Editorial Director, Travel

Publishing for Technology Dummies

Andy Cummings, Vice President and Publisher, Dummies Technology/General User

Composition Services

Gerry Fahey, Vice President of Production Services

Debbie Stailey, Director of Composition Services

Introduction

If you've picked up this book, you've got some big dreams for expanding your business. And your dreams go beyond Canada's borders. Exporting your product or service to sell in other countries could be a great business move, and this book can help you get serious about the international marketplace. *Canadian Exporting For Dummies* separates the myths from the realities and guides you through your export venture.

Whether you're a new exporter who's just starting out, or you're still at the planning stage of your exporting venture, this book can help you figure out where you want your goods or services to go, and how to get them there.

About This Book

These days, it seems that practically everyone and their grandmother is going global, but that doesn't make the notion of expanding your business any less daunting. That's where *Canadian Exporting For Dummies* comes in.

This is a no-nonsense guide for the Canadian exporter to help you formulate your exporting plans, put them into action, and even before all that, know if you're ready to export. From choosing a target market to thinking about the risks involved, *Canadian Exporting For Dummies* gives you lots of information in one convenient package.

Foolish Assumptions

This book assumes a few things about you, the reader:

- ✔ You're a savvy Canadian businessperson with a small- to medium-sized company that provides a product or service.

- ✔ Your business is doing pretty well (pat yourself on the back!).

> ✔ You're interested in expanding your business into the global marketplace — exporting your product or service.
>
> ✔ You're not entirely sure what's involved in exporting, and you're not sure what the rules are.
>
> ✔ You think outside the box — or the country, that is, and you think you're ready to explore international markets.

How This Book Is Organized

So you're making big plans, or starting to make them, anyway. Well, we've written this book with a plan in mind, too. We've organized *Canadian Exporting For Dummies* into four main sections to take you through the various stages of the export journey.

Part 1: Getting Started

In many endeavours, getting started is often the biggest hurdle to overcome. This part asks some pretty fundamental and important questions so you really know what you're getting into. Are you ready to export? And what is your target market?

Once you think you're ready, this book tells you about doing market research (which you probably already know something about), putting your export plan together, thinking about marketing and promotion, and getting your finances in order.

Part 11: Inside the Marketplace

At this point, you're a little deeper in the export venture than you were when you read the previous part. The go-getter in you is probably itching to take action!

This part tells you about the ways you can enter your target market and explains how you can make the process easier on yourself with the help of an intermediary. You also find out about the big issue: Money. Risks are involved in any type of business, so this book looks at some of these risks. You also explore the Big Kahuna of the global marketplace, the United States, and some of the issues you need to consider if that's where you're planning to export. And, because we're living in the age of technology, the book devotes a whole chapter to e-business and how it works to make your export business more efficient and successful.

Part III: Meeting Standards and Keeping It Legal

Knowing the rules and regulations by which exporters must abide can be a tricky business. Although this part doesn't go through everything you need to know (that's a whole other book, after all), it does get you started thinking about international standards and contracts. This part also gives you the lowdown on intellectual property and why protecting your creation is so important.

Part IV: The Part of Tens

The chapters in this section get right to the point. They help you find places to get help with your exporting venture. Also, you get a rundown on the eight big steps of exporting — nothing you can't handle, right?

Icons Used in This Book

As you flip around the pages of this book, a few icons in the left margins are probably going to grab your attention. Great! That's exactly what those icons are for. Here are the icons this books uses and what they mean:

Don't worry, you don't have to fork over 15 percent every time you see this icon (you're saving up money for your exporting venture, anyway). When you do come across it, all that means is you've found a useful bit of information that not everyone knows, and the tip could really help your export business.

Sit up straight and pay attention when you see this little guy. This icon signifies that you're reading information that's very important to know and to always keep in mind, so don't pass over it if you can help it.

This icon doesn't come with flashing red lights or sirens, but the word itself speaks volumes. When you see a warning icon we're informing you of potential pitfalls; if you can avoid them you'll save yourself a headache or two.

Where to Go from Here

Ah, the big existential question! But not at all difficult to answer, because from this point, you're in the driver's seat: You can go anywhere you want.

If this is the first book you've read about exporting, you may feel more comfortable starting from the beginning of the book and reading straight through to the end. At some point, you may also want to check out the handy Appendix of exporting terms, to help you talk the talk as you walk the walk.

However, if you've got a burning question about a specific topic, go ahead and skip to that part, then go back, and then go forward again. *Canadian Exporting For Dummies* is a comprehensive guide that you can read in any order.

And, for additional information, you can visit the Export Development Canada's Web site at www.edc.ca or Team Canada Inc.'s site at exportsource.ca or any of the other great Web sites this book suggests. Have fun and happy exporting!

Part I
Getting Started

"First Harry exported bowling balls, so he took up bowling. Then he exported golf clubs so we took up golf. Now he's exporting surgical instruments, and frankly I haven't had a full night's sleep since."

In this part...

So, you're thinking about expanding your domestic business into the global marketplace — in other words, becoming an exporter. But where the heck do you begin?

This part starts you off right by helping you decide if you're ready to export. If you discover that you are, it takes you through some of the first planning stages, such as finding your perfect target market, creating your export strategy, and getting the financing you need to make it all happen.

Chapter 1

How Do I Know If I'm Ready to Export?

. . . .

. . . .

*S*o your business at home has been going well for quite some time and you think you're ready to explore the unknown — to spread your business wings and conquer new markets through the exciting world of exporting. But first, you want some assurance that you're not risking it all only to fall flat on your face.

First you need to consider the pros and cons of taking your business to the international level. You also need to do a bit of soul searching: Know your business, yourself, and whether you're ready to export. This chapter helps you ask the tough questions.

The Pros of Exporting

Your interest is piqued, but before you get any more involved you want to know the answer to that big question: What's in it for me?

Weighing the pros and cons is a good idea when taking on any new venture, so check out this list to see some of the benefits of exporting and how they apply to you.

✔ **Increased competitiveness:** If you go global successfully, you can compete with the best of 'em. That means that your product, and your business, is among the best in the world. What better security than to know that you'll always be able to compete with foreign companies in your own country?

✔ **International experience:** You're not the only one going global! Foreign companies are exporting to Canada, Canada is exporting to foreign companies ... goods and services are being exchanged all over the world. Gaining international experience is a great way to keep both your company and Canada competitive in the international marketplace.

✔ **Lower costs:** By this point in your business career, you certainly understand the benefits of mass production. As your production levels rise, your production costs, per product, fall. The more demand that exists for your product and the more places you have to sell to, the more goods you have to produce!

✔ **More sales and higher profits:** Your product is already flying off the shelves, or at least enjoying a steady flow at the check-out counter at home. For all you know, your product is rare outside of Canada. Supplying your goods on the international marketplace can significantly bump up your sales, and your business will reap the financial benefits.

✔ **More stability:** As a business owner, you're likely aware that your company's profits depend on the local marketplace. Market downturns could have a potentially devastating effect on your business. If you diversify by selling your goods or services on an international scale, a downturn in one market won't hurt your business as much, because you're still making money in other strong markets. Relying on the economies of many markets, rather than just one, balances out your business.

✔ **New ideas and knowledge:** The best way to learn new business techniques is to step out of your old comfy domestic running shoes and into a pair with an international flair! Selling your goods or services abroad exposes you to new ideas and new ways of doing business. You don't have to change everything you've been doing, but the knowledge that comes with selling to an international marketplace may give you innovative ideas for your business at home.

The Cons of Exporting

Like any difficult decision, you must certainly look at negatives before taking a big leap, and exporting is no exception. Luckily, if you take these factors into consideration before going international, you'll be prepared to meet them head-on.

- ✔ **Bureaucracy and paperwork:** Ah, governments and their love of paperwork! If you already feel that your domestic business is drowning in paperwork, you may want to make a more efficient system, because both the Canadian and foreign governments are pretty demanding when it comes to documenting goods and services from exporters.

- ✔ **Higher costs:** Sure, "The Pros of Exporting" section reminds you that you can make a lot more money by expanding, but you're a businessperson; you know that to make money, you have to spend money. Expanding your business into the international market means bearing extra costs. You will have to spend more on hiring market experts, researching markets, understanding customs and packaging, travelling to and from your target market, and producing more goods.

- ✔ **Huge commitment:** Chances are if you put in the time to start up your own business at home, you're well aware of the commitment it takes to expand your business. Other areas of your life may have to be put on hold because you will have to work long hours and put your blood, sweat, and tears into the venture. Also, you might have to wait anywhere from months to years to begin seeing the profits that you really want to get out of your export investment.

- ✔ **Less time for yourself:** Business is built on personal relationships and trust. Many foreign customers expect to spend face-to-face time with senior people in your business, which could be you. So be prepared to invest your time as well as your money.

- ✔ **Stiff competition:** Facing competitors is a part of business that you can't avoid. Just like when you began your business in Canada, research into the competition is an important aspect of a successful business abroad. Stay on top of the competition so that they don't get on top of you.

None of these difficulties should come as much of a surprise to you. Many of them — like facing tough competition, for example — can even be viewed in a positive light. You and your business become more adaptable, and you gain valuable experience. You may have one more hurdle to get over in the beginning, but exporting certainly offers opportunities to expand both professionally and personally. You get the chance to see the world beyond your front door.

Knowing If You've Got What It Takes

In order to figure out whether or not you're ready to get into exporting, you have to consider a couple of things, both on a personal and a business level.

Start by getting up close and personal. The world outside your doorstep is a pretty big place and one that you need to make certain that you're ready for. So, how do you know if you're ready? Check out the pros and cons lists of exporting that we offer earlier in this chapter to measure your readiness against your reaction. Does one list resonate more with you than another? Are you happy with your current level of success here in Canada, or are you still eager to expand, despite the dangers of taking on new risks, more work, and new challenges? If your gut reaction is to hide under your domestic covers after your initial assessment, you might want to keep your operation safe and sound at home for a while longer. If you're excited about the pros and even more excited about the challenges that the cons will bring, then you've got the personality to be an exporter.

Before you turn your back on the world beyond your doorstep remember that it is much more accessible than it ever used to be. With the advent of global technology, the world is at your fingertips in ways that your exporting forefathers and foremothers would've given their right arms for... or at least sold them if the asking price was high enough! Thanks to cellphones, e-mail, and those handy hand-held devices that are all-in-one combos, bringing your business with you is easier than ever. The idea of always being "on" may sound intimidating, but your foreign customers will appreciate you being easily accessible, so be sure you're technologically up-to-date.

If you've got the gusto to be an exporter, let's turn to the business side of things: Do you have the right goods, professionally speaking?

If you want to begin selling to a global market, you need to have a few key things in place: The first, of course, is a marketable good (see Chapter 2). You also need to know your own business, expectations, and resources in-depth to expand from domestic to international (see Chapter 3).

Take an honest look at yourself and your business. Ask yourself these questions:

- ✔ Do I know my exporting goals?
- ✔ Am I open to doing business in new ways?
- ✔ Am I ready to offer the maximum commitment necessary to succeed on the international marketplace?

If you answer "yes" to these questions, you've got the stuff exporters are made of, and this book can help you get started on expanding your business.

Chapter 2

The Marketplace: Understanding the Great Unknown

- -

In This Chapter

▶ Understanding markets

▶ Checking out the types of markets

▶ Deciding on the market that suits your business

▶ Getting to know the Canadian Trade Commissioner Service

▶ Avoiding culture shock

- -

*T*he world marketplace is now like a 24-hour convenience store: It's open all day, every day. With hundreds of countries to consider, the task of figuring out which country and market best suit your product can seem a bit overwhelming. Don't be discouraged — this chapter provides you with some ways of determining where your product will be best received.

What's a Market?

Just for a minute, let's go back to Marketing 101. A *market* is a place where goods and services are bought and sold. Every country — in fact, every region of every country — can have its own distinct market. *Supply and demand* (how much of a certain product exists versus how many people want the product) is an element that defines markets.

The people who inhabit a particular area (or marketplace) determine demand. This means that the characteristics of a region — the general needs and wants of its people, including their income levels — comprise the qualities of a market.

Examining Market Types

Before you venture into the global marketplace, you need to understand what's out there. This section looks at three different types of markets to help you determine which market type is the best match for your business. We also cover the qualities that you, as an exporter, need to do business in each type of market. This section provides you with a good starting point to know which type you'd like to focus on and to narrow down your market research.

Here are the three types of markets:

- ✔ **Type 1, strong, competitive economies:** Areas such as the United States, Western Europe, Australia, and Singapore belong to this type. As an exporter to this market, you need to deliver your product and services efficiently; have high quality assurance; provide after-sale services and performance guarantees; and have an in-depth and well-rounded marketing plan.

- ✔ **Type 2, moderately competitive economies:** India, Malaysia, and some South American countries belong to this type. These economies are often based on good relationships. As an exporter to this type of marketplace, you must have excellent interpersonal communication skills; be sensitive to cultural differences; and possess or have access to linguistic fluency.

Asian economies, which are big markets for Canadian exporters, are quite varied. Japan and China are economically strong and hugely competitive (Type 1). But other countries such as Thailand and the Philippines are more challenging and may fit Type 2 or Type 3, depending on their current situation.

- ✔ **Type 3, International Financial Institution (IFI)-funded economies:** Countries in Africa belong to this type of market. An exporter focusing here must be adaptable and flexible. You have to keep up with the politics of the market, too, because they change quickly. You also benefit tremendously from experience working with third-party funding organizations, such as the Canadian International Development Agency (www.acdi-cida.gc.ca) or the World Bank (www.worldbank.org).

✔ Patience is key for entering Type 3 markets. Markets generally develop more slowly in these countries than in countries with stronger economies.

Matching your business to the right market type

Now that you know some of the qualities and characteristics of each type of market, look inward. Think about these questions to figure out what market might be best for your business and for you:

✔ How do your personality and your business fit in with each type of market?

✔ Are you interested in learning about cultures that are very different than yours (see "Culture Shock" at the end of this chapter)?

✔ Are you patient and interested in providing a good or service to a developing country?

✔ Do you prefer to enter directly into a fast-paced environment to match your fast-paced, go-getter personality?

Being honest with yourself about the way you choose to function in a business environment makes this first step much simpler.

Digging deeper into the market types

Defining your target market preference by market type to narrow your search down to a few countries is a good way to begin. But don't forget that countries around the world are just as diverse as your home country (think about the diversity you find in the United States, which we discuss in Chapter 7). Thinking about market segments, which can be characterized by differences in geography, ethnicity, religion, and income, can help you define your target audience. If your product can be divided into *key segments* (specialized areas) — perhaps you make automobiles and you manufacture both luxury cars and minivans — you need to ensure that you're targeting an area that's interested in each key segment that you have to offer. You're hardly going to sell a lot of luxury cars in small-town America, so be region-specific and divide any multiple products you have into distinct parts.

Identifying Your Market through Market Research

After you examine the three types of markets and know which one best suits your business, you're ready to refine your search. Each type of market is quite broad and has some countries that may be more receptive to your product than others. Doing some market research will help you find the best places to export your product.

A little later in this chapter you find out about the two types of research (secondary and primary) that help you gather all the information you need, but first, know what you're looking for.

By performing poor or sloppy market research, you're putting your entire exporting venture at risk and possibly setting yourself up to fail. Be diligent, be precise, and be detailed with your market research to give yourself the best possible chances for success.

Researching your long list of markets

You've learned about types of markets — economically strong, moderately strong, and IFI-funded. Next, whittle down your long list of markets to a shorter one. In a general sense, you can break down international market research into three main steps:

1. **Determining the healthiest markets.** In this first step, pinpoint five to ten possible markets for your good or service and see whether these markets have grown or done poorly. You should also investigate new markets that are just starting up, where you might have fewer competitors.

Although the most logical place to find new markets is in Type 3 markets, because far less industry has been explored in IFI-funded economies, this isn't the only place to explore. Business is often more saturated in Type 1 and 2 markets, but potential exporting opportunities are out there.

Look at the markets you're interested in from your long list of market types, choose three to five, and examine them in detail to see if your good or service can offer something new, or at least be a strong competitor.

2. **Sizing up the markets.** You want to get a thorough picture of the markets you looked at in Step 1. Find out who your competitors are. Discover how big their market shares are.

   Be sure to note what affects the marketing and use of your good or service, such as distribution, differences in culture, or business practices.

3. **Looking at possible trade barriers:** Even if a market appears to be a great match for your product or service, *trade barriers* (such as high import taxes, or policies or laws that might prevent you from exporting goods to a certain country) may exist. (See Chapter 7 for more about trade barriers.)

   Check with the Canadian Trade Commissioner Service (infoexport.gc.ca) to find out what barriers could stand in the way of your exporting business. We tell you more about the Trade Commissioner Service later on in this chapter.

   Canadian and foreign governments may offer incentives to exporters, so find out if any are available that pertain to your good or service. Chapter 5 offers more tips on financing your exporting venture.

4. **Choosing your market(s):** After you've examined the information on your potential target markets, you can decide which market is best for your business. Compare the number of competitors that currently exist within your preferred markets to one another and match this against the things that create demand: population, income, and need. Does it look as though there is room for another competitor? Can you price your goods reasonably while turning the profit that you want? Creating

a system of your business priorities — financial results and personal gains — helps you rank the markets you've identified and narrow your search even further.

Starting small is usually best: Choose only one or two target markets at first, and then move on to new markets once you've had success.

Reading all about it: Secondary research

Your first step is to start with some *secondary research*, which you can do it right from home. Using media such as periodicals, studies, market reports, books, surveys, and statistical analyses, you can gather information on the specifics of the markets that have piqued your interest.

To get started, you can find market information online through any of the following sources (and see Chapter 3 for more):

- ✔ **Export Development Canada (EDC):** With the goal of helping Canadian exporters large and small, EDC provides financing, insurance, and bonding services. EDC is also a great source of valuable foreign market expertise and innovative ideas for serving foreign markets. (www.edc.ca)

- ✔ **ExportSource.ca:** A great source for exporting information online. This Team Canada Inc Web site gives you lots of advice and resources on getting started and developing your export plan. It also provides a tradeshow search and information about export training. (exportsource.ca)

- ✔ **Industry Canada—Trade Team Canada Services Industries:** This Web site helps companies looking for export development opportunities specific to service industries and capital products. (ttcservices.ic.gc.ca/epic/internet/inttcserv.nsf/en/home)

- ✔ **Statistics Canada:** Here you find a broad range of statistical information and data to help you plan and research your exporting venture. (www.statcan.ca)

Seeing it for yourself: Primary research

Pack your bags, 'cause you're going to experience your market first hand! Okay, so *primary research* doesn't *necessarily* involve a trip abroad. You can do your interviews and consultations from your comfy office in Canada to begin with, but chances are, when the time comes to make decisions about what market best suits you, you'll want to have made the trip to foreign soil before making that call.

Contacting potential customers

You can contact potential customers overseas in a couple of ways. If you're the product exporter then, by definition, your customer must be the product importer! Try searching the Internet for import organizations, complete with contact information, to see who already deals in your product. Looking for large-scale organizations that import your good or service is a good starting place: Find out about the existing market and see who's interested in what you have to offer.

Finding out about smaller markets — stores or organizations — that may be interested in your product is a bit more difficult from home, so be nice to the contacts that you make overseas. They may be able to offer you leads on lesser-known customers whom you can approach.

Why start at secondary?

You may wonder why the order of your research seems backwards — that is, why secondary research comes before primary research. Simply put: time and money. Your initial secondary research probably involves some time on the phone with potential foreign customers. After you confirm for yourself which customers in which markets hold your interest, make a personal visit. Visiting all of the places you had in mind from the beginning would be pretty costly, even if you have pared down your list quite a bit. Beginning with secondary research — research from home — saves you an earful of phone conversations and a pocketful of money that you'd spend flying to countries you may never end up doing business in.

Discussing your objectives

You want to create a relationship with a potential customer to encourage future business relations and to ensure that your business relationship is a mutually beneficial one. A good way to do this is to first know your company *objectives* — what revenue you hope to get out of what product or service and over what period of time — and then share the relevant, relationship-forming information with potential foreign customers.

The details of your company's finances are personal but the financial relationship between you and a customer is open business. Start with a brief company description. Give the details that are important in getting them acquainted with who you are and what you do, but don't exhaust them with information that is irrelevant this early on in the game. Convey some basic information:

- The history of your company;
- The industries and markets your company serves, as well as any professional affiliations; and
- The good or service you'll be providing.

Understanding the customer

You've laid out your objectives and your company to a potential customer, now what do *you* want to know? Ask questions and make sure that what you're asking is based on the information you learned in your secondary research.

 Keeping both a list of questions and your market profiling checklist in front of you will help you get more concise and helpful answers to take you forward. You don't want to look like some hack who suddenly decided to export without knowing a thing about the business, the marketplace you're exploring, or the customer with whom you're speaking. You want to convey yourself as the intelligent, business-savvy professional that you are!

A Helping Hand: The Canadian Trade Commissioner Service

The mission of the Canadian Trade Commissioner Service is to increase the number of Canadian exporters and the diversity of this country's exports. So check with them at `infoexport.gc.ca` after you research your target market and know where your exporting business is going. The Trade Commissioner Service has offices across Canada and around the world.

The Trade Commissioner Service offers many useful services to help you get up and running. These include:

- ✔ Expert advice for implementing your export strategy (see Chapter 3)
- ✔ Guidance to financial assistance programs and government funding for your export business (see Chapter 5 for more about financing)
- ✔ Hundreds of market reports on 25 international industry sectors
- ✔ Seminars to give you information about overseas business opportunities.

The Trade Commissioner Service has offices in over 140 international cities. Contact them abroad and they can connect you with foreign contacts and assess your business's export potential.

Register your business with the Trade Commissioner Service to access these services (for free!):

- ✔ Access to personalized information on your target market and industry sector through the Virtual Trade Commissioner Web site;
- ✔ International business leads; and
- ✔ International promotion for your business.

Culture Shock

Doing business in foreign countries isn't as simple as making a business plan (which you're used to and probably quite good at, though Chapter 3 provides you with more tips), packaging your product, and sending it over in a box to be sold worldwide. If all goes well, you'll likely be involved in a fair amount of one-on-one, personal relationships with overseas customers.

Talking the talk

If you know in advance that you want to primarily export your product to France, start learning French. Want to export to Chile? Start learning Spanish. Japan? Start learning Japanese... You get the drift: Doing a fair amount of business in a foreign country is certainly easier if you know the language. Your business environment is automatically enhanced and you have the upper hand over other foreign-business owners who don't know the language and can't carry on the same personal communication as you can.

Being unable to speak fluently doesn't mean you're out of the export business. You have options for communicating, such as hiring a translator as your representative — either in your own country or overseas.

Though people can generally get by with simple hand-gestures, research the country you're exporting to before you go to make sure you don't do anything offensive. One hand-gesture can mean five different things in five different countries.

Visiting foreign markets

The bigger and more diversified your business becomes, the more countries you may be visiting. Keep these ideas in mind before stepping foot on foreign soil:

- ✔ Be humble, culturally sensitive, and willing to learn about the country you're visiting.

- ✔ If speaking your own language, adjust your vocabulary to suit the needs of the people with whom you're speaking. Avoid colloquialism and keep your speech slow, but not insultingly so!

- ✔ Don't have a one-sided conversation. Give-and-take, inter-active dialogue helps you and the person with whom you're speaking understand each other's goals.

- ✔ Don't allow cultural differences to get in the way. Rather, embrace them and learn from them.

Chapter 3

Developing an Export Plan and a Marketing Strategy

. . . .

In This Chapter

▶ Revisiting your domestic business plan

▶ Knowing the elements of an export plan

▶ Developing a market strategy

. . . .

*U*nless you're one of those rare people who stumble upon the perfect business by jumping head-first into the domestic market without a plan, you've likely already had experience in developing a plan specific to your business. This chapter shows you how to take your existing knowledge, expand your current domestic plan into an export plan, and develop a strategy specific to your international market.

Reviewing and Expanding Your Domestic Business Plan

If your domestic business plan is so old that you have to blow the dust off of it to read it over — or if you (gasp!) never had one to begin with — you'd better get cracking; you've got a lot of work ahead of you. Before entering the export business you want to make sure that your present business plan reflects your present domestic operation. Revisiting your business plan may seem like a lot of work when you've already spent so much time immersed in market research (refer to Chapter 2), but doing so is worth it in the end. Knowing the ins and outs of your own business and defining your business approach to marketing is some of the best confidence-building preparation you can do when entering the world marketplace.

 If you don't already have a business plan, or want some tips for updating your old dinosaur, visit the Business Development Bank of Canada (BDC)'s Web site for some helpful tips (www.bdc.ca). You can also check out the *Canadian Small Business Kit For Dummies, 2nd Edition*.

Before assessing your current business plan, be sure that you have a clear idea of your *goals* — both for your domestic operation as well as your exporting operation — as this will give you something to measure your plan against. Your goals should outline how you'll achieve your intended position in your target market(s). Try listing your expectations for market share, revenue, and profit. Then, when reviewing your current business plan, ask yourself some of the following questions as a starting point:

✔ Does my business plan reflect my current domestic operation?

✔ Did I go astray from my original plan in my current operation? If so, where does my current business show improvement over that plan?

✔ What common elements can I carry forward from my domestic business plan to my exporting plan to help me achieve my exporting goals?

✔ Can I remove any elements from my plan that are not applicable to an exporting plan?

Looking at Export Plans

It's true: Even after all that work reviewing your old domestic business plan, you still have more work to do. But all of the work — and thinking — that you do in reviving the original business plan is useful in going that next step: developing your export plan. Your goal is to identify your target market(s) (which you've likely already done, or can do, through the market research techniques outlined in Chapter 2), export goal(s), necessary resources, and anticipated results. So, your export plan is, at its core, a business plan with a special focus on international markets.

Understanding the importance of export plans

Making an export plan is important for two reasons:

- ✓ **Focus:** A plan keeps you focused on your goals and objectives, which makes implementing your plan a heck of a lot easier. You don't want to be running around like chicken with its head cut off when you finally get the ball rolling. You want a well thought-out plan to refer to. It'll keep you grounded if anything unexpected arises in your future export business.

- ✓ **Financing:** An export plan is essential for financing purposes. You want to have something tangible to show to potential investors or to your bank (see Chapter 5 for more information on financing).

Checking out the elements of an export plan

The following is an outline of some main elements to include in your export plan:

- ✓ **Introduction:** This section should include information about the history of your business, as well as its vision and mission statement. Also, state the purpose of your export plan and your short- and long-term goals.

- ✓ **Structure of your business:** In this section, describe the business's ownership, management and staffing structure, and any alliances that will strengthen your market presence. Include any relevant experience the business may have had in exporting ventures.

- ✓ **Products and services:** In this section, describe the products or services that your business offers and their key features. Include information about production methods as well. Describe how you plan to adapt your product or service for new markets or any future products or services you would like to offer.

✔ **Export market:** In this section, include information on the market research you've performed, such as market size, the key segments (refer to Chapter 2) that you're targeting, and any particular political issues that may affect your business. Describe the process and criteria for financial transactions in the target markets and the barriers that you may encounter. Also, describe industry trends and an overall picture of the market's outlook for the future.

✔ **Market-entry strategy:** This section specifies information about your target markets and how you plan to introduce your product to those markets. Describe any notable competitors and how your product or service's position has an advantage. State strategy for pricing, distributing, promoting, and developing sales leads for your product or service. Include information about any intermediaries or partners you may have.

✔ **Regulatory issues:** This section tells how you are protecting your intellectual property and lists any insurance you may need (transportation, cargo). It also includes information on trade documentation and any trade service providers you may be using.

✔ **Risks:** In this section provide information on market risks, credit and currency risks, political risks, or any other risks that apply to your specific situation.

✔ **Finances:** This section states the sources of funding and revenue that you have available. It also gives the cost of sales, marketing and promotional costs, and any other expenses your exporting business may have. Include your operating budget here, too.

The more complete your export plan, the more this roadmap to success can help your exporting venture to succeed.

Developing a Marketing Strategy

In the business world, remember: *Marketing is strategy*. *Marketing* is the process you use to attract customers to your product and convince them to buy it. In this section, you look at the overall strategic plan: the big picture. In Chapter 4, we talk about putting that plan into action through advertising, sales, and promotion — the tools with which you develop your marketing strategy.

The following questions will get you started thinking about your marketing strategy:

- ✓ **What are the important characteristics of my target market?** This is information you gather from market research. (In Chapter 2 we tell you how to make lists about your target markets and their characteristics.)

- ✓ **What marketing approach do my competitors take?** What can I learn from both the successes and the missteps of my competitors to adequately differentiate my business?

- ✓ **What promotional techniques will best reach my market?** (See Chapter 4 for more information on promoting your good or service.)

- ✓ **In what ways should I modify my existing marketing materials — or even my product or service itself — to better suit this new market?**

Just like your operation at home, your business abroad is subject to the ups and downs and changing trends of the local market. This is why staying on top of your marketing strategy at all times is important. See your strategy as something fluid, just like the world marketplace.

You can communicate to the public and sell them your product or service in many ways. Your strategy comprises many different components, including determining the mode of delivery, price, and promotion. In order to arrive at those decisions, a lot of pre-work is required, which we talk about in the following sections.

Knowing the essentials of marketing internationally

Any first-year marketing course tells you the four P's of marketing:

- ✓ **Product:** The good or service you are selling.

- ✓ **Place:** How you distribute your good or service, and to where you distribute it.

- ✔ **Price:** The way you determine how much your good or service costs.

- ✔ **Promotion:** The ways you let customers know that your good or service is out there and available to them.

After you enter into the international business world, things become more complicated. You have many more elements to consider:

- ✔ **Business partners:** Any partner with whom you are working to help strengthen your business.

- ✔ **Documents:** The legally required documents you must complete in order to ship goods internationally.

- ✔ **Laws:** Standards and procedures for conducting business.

- ✔ **Payment:** The tricky parts involved when money is exchanged internationally.

- ✔ **Precautions:** The steps you have taken to protect your business and its intellectual property from potential risks.

- ✔ **Product positioning:** The manner in which you want to be seen in the marketplace.

- ✔ **Staff:** If you have staff, they must be trained and well-equipped to deal with international transactions.

- ✔ **Systems and customs:** The differences in business practices from your culture to the culture you're dealing with.

Why keep all these elements in mind? Control. Your business is always affected by the internal and external characteristics of the environment that you're targeting. On an international scale, you deal with more unknown factors and have more elements to consider than you would on a local scale.

Finding information on your target market

Chapter 2 tells you all about how to identify your target market. So by now, you may have identified the type of market that best fits your business and may have even chosen something location-specific, but the question of how to get down to the nitty-gritty details of a foreign market remains.

Check out some of these sites, where you can register your Canadian business to get leads on international opportunities:

- ✔ **IFInet:** This is a site for International Trade Canada. Here you will find information on procurement processes and investment criteria of multilateral development banks, bilateral development agencies, and United Nations agencies. (www.infoexport.gc.ca/ifinet)

- ✔ **SourceCAN:** Matches Canadian products and services with thousands of domestic and foreign business opportunities, both on the corporate and government level, and... it's free! (www.sourcecan.com)

- ✔ **Virtual Trade Commissioner:** Provides you with market information, business opportunities, and the ability to make service requests with a focus on smaller countries and niche markets of a manageable size. (infoexport.gc.ca)

Looking at the parts of a marketing plan

If you've already made your export plan (refer to "Looking at Export Plans"), then your brain is working on the right track. An *exporting marketing plan* is your plan that outlines how you will tell potential customers about your product or service and convince them to buy it.

- ✔ **Evaluation of your product or service:** Clearly describe your product or service. Pat yourself on the back by listing, realistically, its unique selling points and brainstorm ways it may be marketable internationally.

- ✔ **Evaluation of the market:** Get deep into the size and trends of your target markets. What are the key economic, social, political, and cultural characteristics of your market? Put yourself in the shoes of your target customer — their buying patterns and purchasing decisions. Check out Chapter 2 for techniques on researching your target market.

- ✔ **Competition study:** Check out the competition and figure out what position your good or service might slide into.

✔ **Goals:** We talk about defining your goals earlier in this chapter. Keep them in mind at all times to ensure that the reason behind everything you do is to meet those goals.

✔ **Technical issues:** What's your mode of delivery? Your pricing recommendations? Promotional methods?

✔ **Execution:** You've got it all down in theory, now get specific. What activities will you undertake to carry out your marketing strategy? List dates and names of people responsible for acting out these activities. Refer to your export plan to make sure you're always on track with your goals. See Chapter 6 for more information on putting your plan into action.

✔ **Assessment tools:** Create a system to continuously test yourself throughout your new business endeavour. How will you measure whether or not you're achieving your goals?

✔ **Concluding summary:** Bring the whole plan together by summing up the ways that the goals of your marketing plan will fit your overall export plan.

Staying in check

Keep asking yourself a few key questions throughout your exporting business venture and you'll keep yourself, and your marketing strategy, in place.

✔ What is the nature of my industry?

✔ Who is my target customer — where are they, and have they changed since I first began my exporting business?

✔ Is my company's marketing strategy still applicable to my current market?

✔ Is the current market still applicable to my product?

✔ Is the price of my good or service still appropriate?

✔ Is my marketing material — advertising and promotional information — doing all that it can do to convey the desired image of my company?

Chapter 4

Pricing and Promoting Your Goods

*A*lthough you're obviously passionate about your business and eager to expand and share it with the world, you have another pretty strong motive for undertaking this exciting export venture: making money. And hey, that's okay (since you're a businessperson, you probably already know that).

This chapter takes you through the laws of supply and demand, examines the eternal mystery of pricing strategies, and helps you check out the competition. It also tells you what options are available to you for promoting your product.

Is the Price Right?

A number of factors go into the actual practice of selling your goods. You have to thoroughly think through pricing and competition, and then you have to shell out the cash for promotion. Remember the old adage: You have to spend money to make money. If you do everything right, you drastically increase the chances of your investment offering a satisfactory (or hopefully exceptional!) return. But before you get to the return on investment portion of your business, you have to understand a few basic points about economics: the laws of supply and demand and competition. Then, you can find the best strategy for pricing your goods.

Looking at supply and demand

Supply and demand (the amount of a particular good available and the amount of consumers who want the good) is likely not a new concept to you, since you've already had to price your good or service domestically. So what's different now? Well, you probably began with a pretty solid base of understanding the Canadian marketplace — how much the market could bear to support you — when you priced your product domestically. If you want to go international, you have to consider the same laws of supply and demand, but in a market you know very little or nothing about.

So get out your research hat again, because you're going to need a rather in-depth knowledge in order to price your goods. Start by answering these questions:

- ✔ What is the demand for the product I'm offering?
- ✔ What is the competitive landscape in my target market?
- ✔ What are local import laws and custom requirements in my target market?

Most of this information should become apparent during your market research stage (refer to Chapter 2). Chapter 8 provides further tips on how to research the laws and custom requirements of your target market.

In most places, demand is most affected by *per-capita income*, which is the average income per person (you divide the total income of your market by the total population of your market to figure it out). Industrialized countries generally function at similar per-capita incomes, which means your knowledge of the Canadian, and possibly American, marketplace acts as a good starting point. The more money people make, the more they have to spend. If you're selling in non-industrialized countries, the per-capita income is much lower, so generally, demand is lower too.

Of course, exceptions always exist. Occasionally, a product or service is in such high demand that the relative wealth of the country has little to no effect on the selling price of your good. For example, people generally have to buy toilet paper. So while the manufacturers certainly aren't demanding fifty bucks a roll, they do have a fair amount of control over the price of the good. The target market isn't going to stop buying toilet paper if the price is raised significantly. In this case, however, the many toilet paper manufacturers keep its price in check — thank goodness for competition!

How do you know how much you can charge for your product or service? Assessing whether the product is a necessity or a luxury helps you set a price. If it's a luxury, think about the following questions:

✔ How appealing is it?

✔ How many people will want it?

✔ How often will people want it?

✔ How much are people willing to pay for it?

Deciding on a price

You can't price your product or service by pulling a number out of thin air. As with all the other elements of export planning, you have many factors to take into account when deciding on a price.

The golden rule of settling on a final price is that, above all, you must think strategically. Other than supply and demand, which we discuss earlier in this chapter, here are some more factors you need to consider (you may have others, depending on your good or service):

✔ **Changes and tweaks:** You may have to modify your products or service in some way before you sell it in a foreign market (you may need to create packaging with bilingual instructions, for example).

✔ **Insurance:** You may need to buy extra insurance or a special type of insurance, depending on what you're exporting.

✔ **Marketing costs:** You know you can't quietly slip your product into the marketplace and expect sales. How much are you willing to spend on marketing (refer to Chapter 3) to let potential customers know your product is available? These costs probably won't be the same in a foreign market as they are domestically.

✔ **Production costs:** This is a big one. Production costs vary depending on what you're selling. They can be very high and complicated to determine (such as if many small components go into making the electric heaters you export) or more simple (if you export handmade mittens).

✔ **Profit objectives:** Think about the objectives you defined for yourself in Chapter 2. Are you jumping into a new market or looking to grow within an established market? Do you want to make a lot of money right away, which may require spending more at first? Or are you expecting to start smaller and get modest profits that you increase over time?

✔ **Salaries or commissions for staff:** Expanding your business probably means hiring more staff, perhaps to work overseas.

✔ **Shipping and distribution:** Your product or service has a lot farther to go to reach an overseas market. You can ship your product in different ways (see Chapter 6 for more), some of which cost more than others.

✔ **The competition's prices:** Researching the competition's prices is just as important for export markets as it is for domestic markets. Familiarizing yourself with the economy of your target market is a start, but be sure to get into the specifics of who else has either established a space in, or is fighting for a space in, your market. You either have to match or undercut competitor prices to stake your claim in the market share.

Common mistakes to avoid are pricing your good or service only according to your production costs, or only according to the competition's prices. Before setting a price, list all your business's costs and even try to estimate future costs.

✔ **Travel costs:** You may be travelling a lot farther to get to meetings than you used to! Predict how often you'll visit your target market, or send staff there.

After you start itemizing the factors that have an effect on your product's price, you might not be able to stop! But after you list all the elements you can think of, ultimately the price you set for your product must be competitive. If your granola bars are five times the price of other granola bars in the target market, will anyone be willing to pay for them?

Checking Out Forms of Promotion

After you develop and implement an export strategy, look at various forms of promotion. Promoting your goods in the manner that they deserve is key to expanding your business successfully.

Consider the following tried and true forms of promotion:

- ✔ **Advertising:** Be sure to advertise in both the right form of media and with the right message (seems that Marshall McLuhan really knew his stuff). Your ad needs to speak to your target audience and it has to reach them. Should you advertise luxury cars at a bus stop? Probably not.

- ✔ **Business trips:** Nothing is like a good old-fashioned handshake to begin a good old-fashioned face-to-face meeting. It works in your favour if you can spend a certain amount of time in the country you'll be exporting to, getting to know the local ways, and forming interpersonal connections with your overseas customers.

- ✔ **Direct mail:** This method can be very effective for reaching your target market. Be sure to do your research first, however, because sending customized mailing packages to uninterested parties is pointless. Sending a brochure for your dating service to a married couple probably won't get a great response. Direct mail is only effective if you put in the effort beforehand. Research, customize, and then send!

- ✔ **Logo and slogan:** A slick-looking logo and catchy slogan really help your product or service stick in potential customers' minds. They also help to *brand* (give a distinct identity to) your business.

- ✔ **Marketing materials**: These may include anything from glossy brochures to pens with your company name on them.

The marketing materials that work in your domestic market may not be appropriate for the international marketplace you'll be working in. Examine them closely in the context of everything that you know about the culture of your new target market (see Chapter 2) and seriously consider whether or not the material may be offensive, inappropriate, or just plain meaningless to your new audience. The last thing you want is promotional material that falls so flat it simply doesn't promote.

If you're entering a non-English-speaking market, factor in the cost of translation — and be sure to hire a translator that has experience in business writing.

✔ **Media coverage:** You can establish your presence pretty quickly through media exposure, if you can get it. Find the medium that your buyers are most interested in, prepare a media kit that profiles your company's mission, your product or service, and all of the good things that your company has done, and then put it out to establish credibility. Send press releases to local media outlets and to let them know you're in town.

Have any translated materials double-checked by someone from the country you're marketing to before sending them out. And never rely on those quick online translators, which can produce some real doozies! You don't want your promotional material to become one of those hilarious translation blunders you see on the Internet, do you?

✔ **Trade shows:** Everything under one sun, what more could the busy businessperson ask for? Trade shows are so multi-faceted that they can save you time in other areas of your business. You can promote your business, do market research, and eye the competition all at once.

The costs of participating in a trade show could be fairly minimal. Consider things such as the cost of buying and setting up a booth, employing staff (or yourself) to work the show if it's non-business hours, and committing office hours in advance of the show to planning your participation, but the exposure and diversity of results could be well worth it.

Trade shows are great opportunities to network. And who knows? Maybe someone you thought was competition can wind up being a partner in your next business venture.

✔ **Web presence:** If you don't yet have a Web site set up for your business, you might want to get with the times! This is one place worthy of investing some money. The Internet abounds with promotional opportunity. Setting up a company Web site is pretty simple, but doing it right is integral. Hiring someone to design your site on the cheap, or failing to update an existing, outdated site may do more harm than good. You want a well-composed site to represent your business and your product.

Sharpening Your Marketing Tools

Knowing what forms of promotion best suit your product is the first step to getting the exposure you need, but knowing the ins and outs of each marketing tool is crucial to making sure that the exposure you're getting is representing you to your maximum potential.

We list a few marketing tools that you may already be using to promote your business at home. You may not currently use all of these items, but if you do now — or might in the future — think about how to make the most of them:

- **Bios of key players:** So what if you're the only one? Toot your own horn and create a short biography that lists your accomplishments to impress potential customers. You could include a photograph with your bio, but be sure that a professional takes the photo. The snapshot of you at your sister's birthday party simply won't do.

- **Brochures:** Do you think they communicate the essential elements of your business to someone who has just been introduced to it? Be sure that brochures are on good quality paper and look creative to distinguish them from other brochures. Also, be sure they contain up-to-date contact information!

- **CD-ROMs and DVDs:** You may consider having a CD-ROM professionally produced that shows your product or service. It can look impressive and adds a bit of fun to your promotional material. Do be sure they look professional, however. Your overseas customers won't want to listen to stiff narration or bad acting any more than your domestic customers.

- **Customer testimonials:** Contact some of your satisfied customers (although you probably have so many that choosing will be difficult). Ask them to write a letter of reference for you, or to write a letter describing their positive experiences with your business. If you know people in high-profile positions (a president of a company, for example) their testimonials might impress potential customers, too.

✔ **Letterhead and business cards:** We don't mean to sound superficial here, but looks *do* matter. Be sure they're of high quality, clear, and visually appealing.

✔ **Media publicity:** If any newspapers or magazines have mentioned your product or service (in a positive way, of course), save those clippings and show them off!

✔ **Product sample:** You'll probably give or show samples of your product to potential customers. Check the product a million times before sending it out to ensure it isn't faulty.

✔ **Web site:** You don't need a fancy intro, but your Web site does need to look professional and be easy to navigate. Update it as often as possible.

If you have some of the tools of marketing we outline, you should assemble them into a slick-looking promotional package or media kit. Use a folder with your company logo on the cover. Include your brochures, copies of newspaper or magazine articles about your company, letters of reference from satisfied customers, and anything else that shows off how great your business is. Pass out the package to potential foreign customers so they can see how great your business is doing domestically and keep it as reference.

A product by any other name . . .

Your product's name and your business's name create the image you want to present to customers. If you must translate your product or business's name for a foreign-language market, be sure to double-check, triple-check (heck, even quadruple-check!) the name's meanings in the other language. (Or have someone do it for you, if you're not able.) Imagine what a disaster it would be to go through all the trouble of setting up your exporting venture, only to find out that your translation of "luxurious face cream" is also a slang for "head like a giant lizard's" in the local culture. The last thing you want is a business image, name, or product name that is offensive or inappropriate in your target market's language.

Chapter 5

Financing Your Exporting Venture

· ·

In This Chapter

▶ Thinking about the financial risks

▶ Making a financial plan

▶ Looking for help with your financing

▶ Knowing the methods of payment

▶ Discovering the formula for success

· ·

*F*inancing a business is likely not a new concept to you. But you're probably thinking that financing an export business is a much, much larger scale than you're used to. It's true: Financing an export business can be risky and complicated, but don't let that get in the way of your dreams. You are, after all, an entrepreneur. If you started a business at home, then you've got the know-how and drive to start one abroad. You just need to understand a few technical details about exporting finance and away you go!

Weighing the Financial Risks

The pros and cons, the good and bad, the yin and yang: Besides thinking about the heaps and heaps of financial benefits you'll (hopefully) reap from your exporting business, you must consider the financial risks you're about to undertake:

> ✔ **Time delay on delivery of goods:** As a kid, you may have learned the hard way that digging a hole to Asia is impossible (or at least would take a really, really long time), so

remember that shortcuts rarely exist between you and an overseas customer. You're likely fairly far away from your export market, and between the time you ship out your goods and the time they actually arrive at their destination, anything can happen (refer to Chapter 6 for information about protecting your goods in transit).

✔ **Delay on getting paid:** Your overseas customer may ask for 30, 60, or even 90 days to pay you. If that payment period makes your eyes pop out of your head, get used to it — the 30- to 90-day time period isn't unreasonable in the export business. If you're not prepared for the delay, you might experience cash flow problems.

Because not getting paid is a risk that you must always consider (see "Protecting yourself against non-payment" later in this chapter), self-financing a growing export business isn't necessarily a good idea, particularly if your business is small or very new.

✔ **Risks of success:** You've just received a huge international order. That's great news that means your first step into the export world is a positive one, but you somehow need to cover the time in between manufacturing and delivering this giant order, and receiving money for it.

Financing for your foreign customers

Good news: As a new exporter, you can go through Export Development Canada (EDC) to offer foreign customers loans and flexible financing terms.

If your foreign customer has a solid financial record, they might qualify for a loan from EDC or one of their financial partners. Check out www.edc.ca/edcfinancing. We tell you more about EDC later in this chapter, too.

Planning Out Your Export Finances

A 2004 KPMG study compared the costs of doing business in 11 industrial countries, including the G7 countries. It found that Canada was the least expensive of those countries in which to conduct business. That's the good news. The bad news is that "least expensive" doesn't mean cheap, and the costs of exporting can still be pretty high when you begin to add them all together.

The best way to combat the high costs and risks of exporting is to simply be prepared for them. You want to start out with a wide-ranging financial plan. Don't just plan for what *should* happen, but take into account what *could* happen (take a look at the previous section for some risks you might face).

Entering a new market in a foreign country means that you're facing a lot of unknown factors. You want to be certain of strong financial stability, stemming from a reliable cash flow, so that when problems arise, you can face them head on because you've already planned for them. That way, dealing with problems is easier, and problems don't bring your business's momentum to a halt.

A budget is also helpful for keeping your finances in check. Although you might not always be able to stick to it, having your financial budget planned out gives you something concrete to refer to, to keep yourself in check.

Understanding the importance of planning cash flow

After all that export planning (refer to Chapters 2 and 3) and marketing planning (refer to Chapters 3 and 4) that you've done, you're growing tired of laying out plans. But thinking about your *cash flow* (the money that comes in and goes out of your business) in advance is important. When do you expect to make money, and when do you expect to have to pay money? Planning your cash flow helps you to defend against:

- ✔ Customers who pay slowly (or not at all)
- ✔ Fluctuations in exchange rates
- ✔ Natural disasters
- ✔ Political events

Your business profits (how much money the business makes) is not always the best indicator of your business's overall wellbeing. Of course you love to see what money is coming in the door, but if you don't also watch what's going out, your business might be in trouble. Because you have all sorts of new expenses as an exporter, paying attention to these expenses is especially important.

Because you can't predict turnaround time for buyer payments, you want to be sure that your company always has access to either cash or an operating line of credit. Both serve the same function, which is to act as a cushion to keep your business afloat until you get paid.

Cash flow planning is a continuous activity and an important tool for keeping your business financially sound. It allows you to see when those pesky expenses are getting out of line!

Making budgets

Successful business owners never stop thinking about and adjusting their business's *budget* (a document or spreadsheet that outlines all of your business's planned expenses). Considering and monitoring your budget becomes especially important when you enter into exporting, because you've suddenly got a lot of new costs to deal with. Include the following two types of budgets in your overall financial plan:

- ✔ **A cash budget:** Your cash budget outlines your financing requirements for the next two or three years. This allows you to determine the timing and the amounts of cash that you spend. Essentially, it comes down to this: When will you receive cash and when will you pay your bills? Don't confuse the theory with the practice. You're not predicting sales and expenses, but rather looking at when the money from sales and allotted to expenses will come and go.

You've probably made a cash budget when you set up your business at home. As a refresher, here's what you need to complete:

- **A balance sheet:** A snapshot of your business's financial position at a given time.

- **An operating forecast:** This tracks all of your business's financial activities. It tracks monthly income and outflow.

- **A timeline:** This element summarizes the balance sheet and operating forecasts and pinpoints the times at which your financial activities occur.

If you need a refresher course on budget planning or if your old worksheets are out of date, pick up a business book, or have a glance at the *Canadian Small Business Kit For Dummies, Second Edition.*

✔ **A capital budget:** If your cash budget is for day-to-day operations, think of your capital budget as a long-term plan. Your capital budget details all long-term funds that you need for your export project, such as the cost of acquiring new equipment or expanding a factory. It provides a plan to measure the expenditures you need for long-term expansion, and shows how much increased cash flow will be needed to justify those expenditures.

Finding Financial Services for Exporters

At the beginning of this chapter, we tell you that self-financing is really not the best or safest way to fund your exporting business (check out "Weighing the Financial Risks") — so you're wondering where to turn to. We discuss two good sources to look to for financial assistance and information in this section.

Export Development Canada (EDC)

EDC provides finance, insurance, and bonding solutions to Canadian companies exporting to or investing in foreign countries. Operating in 200 markets worldwide (including 130 emerging markets) EDC's aim is to help Canadian companies manage risk and gain the maximum benefits from global trade opportunities. They offer a number of programs and services to help finance or minimize the risks involved in your export venture.

The *Pre-shipment Financing Program* encourages your bank to give you a loan to finance your work-in-progress needs by providing a guarantee to your bank that covers up to 75 percent of the loan value.

EDC can also provide direct loans to your foreign customer. Or, they provide insurance, which can cover up to 90 percent of your losses if your buyer doesn't pay. The insurance can also be used as security so your bank can extend your working capital.

How can EDC offer you even more security? They have a number of services. For instance, they can help if your buyer requires you to post a bond to guarantee your bid or perform-ance, and can work with your bank or surety company to provide financial guarantees.

Check out www.edc.ca or call 1-800-650-2338 to find out more about EDC's products and services.

Business Development Bank of Canada (BDC)

BDC is a financial institution that is owned by the Canadian government. Their aim is to provide financial, investment, and consulting services to Canadian small businesses, with a special focus on exporting. They offer long-term financing and flexible payment schedules, along with expertise in Canadian small business export financing.

BDC can help you to:

- ✔ Perform market research
- ✔ Develop international markets
- ✔ Make product modifications to tailor your product to international markets
- ✔ Purchase new, technologically advanced equipment to improve production

You may even qualify for their specialized *Innovation Financing*: up to $250,000 for innovative businesses to access new markets and technologies. Check BDC out at www.bdc.ca or call 1-877-232-2269.

Getting Paid

After all that work, and all that worry, and all of the various plans that you've put down on paper and executed, you want to get paid. Your international customers can pay you using a few different methods, some of which are more secure than others. The less secure the method of payment, the more you need to know about how to protect your business against non-payment.

Knowing how customers can pay you

Be aware of all the methods of payment in advance of doing an export deal. Of course, you may already have your preference in mind for what kind of deal you want to make with a customer for payment. To get to know your options, check out the list below — it ranges from the most secure type of payment to the least secure type of payment.

- ✔ **Cash up front:** You know that you're reliable, but you don't necessarily know that your customer is reliable. What could put your fears to rest better than getting payment before you've even delivered the goods?

If you can swing it, advance payment is definitely the way to go. It completely eliminates the risk of non-payment. Cash up front also gives you money to work with, so your business has more flexibility if you have to deal with other customers who may not be able to provide money in advance.

Although the cash-in-advance method is the best option for you, you might be hard pressed to find customers willing to go this route — it really poses no advantage for them. Try splitting the difference between full payment up-front and waiting until the goods are delivered to receive your payment by asking your customers to pay a portion in advance for specially ordered goods or services. Consider asking for a retainer (an up-front fee that covers future services) when you sign a contract for services.

✔ **Letter of credit:** *Letters of credit* (also known as LCs) use an official third party — a bank — to guarantee payment. The guarantee significantly reduces any feelings of vulnerability involved in your export transaction, both for you and for your customer. Although cash in advance might be the best solution for you, the seller, a letter of credit is a more likely possibility. It provides a certain sense of security to both parties involved in the exchange of goods. It is issued on behalf of the buyer (your customer or the LC applicant) and the issuing bank is generally located in the buyer's country (the seller visits an advising bank, located in their own country). The issuing bank confirms that the seller has fulfilled the requirements of the LC. Letters of credit come in two forms:

  • **Confirmed:** A Canadian bank can confirm a foreign bank's letter of credit. This is the best option for you, as seller, because the Canadian bank is agreeing to pay you even if the foreign bank doesn't pay them.

  • **Unconfirmed:** Obviously, this is less preferable, as you're relying on all other parties to make payment so that your bank can pay you.

You can also make your letter of credit *irrevocable*, which means your approval is required for it to be cancelled or altered in any way.

A confirmed *and* irrevocable letter of credit offers you the most security.

A lot of little technicalities can mess things up. Be sure the LC contains no discrepancies, that the name and address are spelled correctly, that the shipping date is right, and that all charges are included. You may be unable to collect from the buyer's bank if these elements aren't correct.

✓ **Documentary credit:** Documentary credit is similar to an LC. Two types exist:

- You can use a *sight* draft to receive payment on sight; meaning, when you present the draft to the bank.

- You can use a *term* documentary credit to allow payments to occur over a period of days — 30, 60, 90, or at a future specified date.

✓ **Documentary collection:** Here's how documentary collection works: You, the exporter, ship your goods to your customer, the importer. You forward the shipping documents to a collecting bank. In order to get a hold of the shipping documents, your customer must pay the collecting bank. After they've done this, you get the money from the collecting bank.

Though it sounds straightforward, the biggest risk in this transaction is your inadvertent exposure to your customer's credit. If the customer can't pay the bank, then the bank can't pay you because the bank made no advance guarantee to pay you.

Much less security exists in a documentary collection than in other bank-aided transactions.

✓ **Open account:** This is by far the riskiest form of payment. Before any form of payment is made to you, you're required to ship the goods to your customer. Open account terms can allow 30, 60, or 90 days (and in some cases longer!) for payment to come due. You're exposed to the credit risk of your customer. Essentially, you're paying for the whole transaction for a long time, which is best to avoid for the security of your business. Doing so can hurt your cash-flow situation and throw your budget out of whack (which we talk about earlier in this chapter).

Protecting yourself against non-payment

The very words "non-payment" are enough to send shivers down the spines of most businesspeople. Of course, non-payment is one of the biggest dangers of the export business — or any self-run business, really. You run this risk enough in your domestic business, but at home you're likely diversified enough to not have to rely on income from one customer (we talk about how diversifying your business is a benefit of exporting in Chapter 1).

Because you can only do so much to ensure that your customers pay you, looking into non-payment insurance is a good idea. Export Development Canada offers accounts receivable insurance that covers up to 90 percent of your loss if your customer can't or won't pay you. Check out www.edc.ca/edcinsurance to find out more about how it can secure your export venture.

Achieving Financial Success

Does a formula for financial success in the exporting business exist? Perhaps. You've heard those stories of people who've found overnight success abroad, and that's great for them. But overnight success isn't something that you — as an experienced businessperson — can rely on, though you can certainly keep it as a pipe dream to get you through our cold Canadian nights.

Instead, keep in mind that the closest thing to a formula for exporting success would be something like this:

Sustained effort + cash investment + long periods of time = Profitable export success.

So you see, nothing magical or mysterious exists here. Just like your mother told you: do something, do it to the best of your abilities, and keep at it!

Part II
Inside the Marketplace

The 5th Wave
By Rich Tennant

"Well, there's another caravan that didn't stop. Something tells me we should have done some market research."

In this part...

*A*fter you research your target market and you know where you're going, your next step is getting your product or service into the target marketplace.

This part looks at some of the practical, hands-on aspects of getting into the marketplace, such as choosing an export method and getting help from intermediaries. It also gives you some special considerations for exporting to our neighbours in the U.S. and takes a look at how e-business can work for you.

Chapter 6

Taking the Plunge: Entering the Market and Managing Your Goods

· ·

In This Chapter

▶ Knowing the methods of market entry

▶ Using an intermediary

▶ Shipping your goods

▶ Delivering your product

· ·

*Y*ou've set your sights on a target market, but what's the best way for you, a foreign exporter, to enter that market? This chapter gives you information about a few options you may want to consider, depending on the size of your business and your personal preferences.

You may also wonder how to put your product into the hands of your international customers. This chapter explores these questions, and also considers more technical issues, such as shipping documentations and permits.

Entering the Market

So, think you're ready to open your target market's door and walk on in? Well, more than one way exists do to this, and you need to decide which is best for you. The upcoming sections discuss the three main means of *market entry* (the ways you introduce your new product or service into your target market) and point out some of the advantages and disadvantages that you need to consider.

We don't cover every means of international market entry in this chapter. You might also be interested in exploring investments, joint ventures, and licensing agreements. For more information about these methods, go to infoexport.gc.ca to find contact information for the regional office of the Trade Commissioner Service nearest you.

Direct exports

If you use the method of *direct exports*, you market and sell your products or services directly to your customers. If your business is very small or you're a hands-on kind of person, this method may work best for you.

Direct exporting works slightly differently depending on whether you're exporting goods or services.

- ✔ **Goods:** You market the goods and sell them directly to the customer.
- ✔ **Services:** You negotiate, contract, and work directly with the customer.

So why might you consider direct exporting as your method of choice? It has several advantages:

- ✔ Your profits might be higher, because you don't have to pay a middleman.
- ✔ You can be more competitive because, with the money you save by doing it all yourself, your prices can be lower.
- ✔ You are in direct contact with your customers. You give them personal attention and personalized service.

Also think about some of the disadvantages of direct exporting:

- ✔ You don't get help from a foreign intermediary, so you're doing all the legwork yourself — and a lot of work at that.
- ✔ You could take a bit longer to familiarize yourself with your target market than you would if you had a foreign intermediary.

✔ Your customers may take longer to warm up to you because you're foreign to them. You need customer trust for your business to succeed.

Indirect exports

Through the *indirect exporting* method, you enter your market through the side door by means of an *intermediary*, someone who's familiar with your target market and who works with you to sell your good or service. (We discuss the different types of intermediaries later on in this chapter.)

The indirect method works differently for goods and for services:

✔ **Goods:** You market and sell to an intermediary, such as a foreign distributor. You can also use a foreign agent or representative who does not directly purchase the goods.

✔ **Services:** You contract with an intermediary who negotiates on your behalf.

Choosing the indirect export method means you're putting part of your business into the hands of someone else. If you're not comfortable with that, or you absolutely have to be in the driver's seat at all times, indirect exporting might not be a good arrangement for you.

However, indirect exporting may be a great way for you to enter your target market, especially if you're a very new exporter. Read more about intermediaries and whether or not this is a good option for you later in this chapter.

Partnerships and alliances

Instead of going it alone, consider forming a partnership in Canada or abroad. Consider the many potential benefits to this arrangement, for both you and the partner:

✔ You and the partner pool your resources and benefit from each other's expertise, insights, and contacts.

✔ You're a team, so you and your partner can focus on your respective business strengths, which could make the venture more enjoyable and successful.

✔ You and the partner share the exporting venture's risks, making it seem less daunting.

✔ You might be able to enter more than one market at once, because you don't have to do all the work alone.

Always think strategy. An easy way to export could be to form a strategic alliance with a business that has a product or service that complements yours. By using the other company's distribution and marketing expertise, your business saves money. Learn more about the different types of partnerships at exportsource.ca.

Consider your partnership carefully; it isn't something you want to enter into lightly. Ask the following questions before forming a partnership:

✔ **Is a partnership right for you and your business?** If a potential partner doesn't offer you anything beyond what you're already capable of doing, give it a pass. But if the partner has expertise you lack or is already connected with your target market, it could be a good match.

✔ **What form and structure do you want the partnership to have?** By considering your company's current strengths and weaknesses, and then seeing how a potential partner could fill in any gaps, you can define a structure that works for both of you.

✔ **Do your goals match those of your potential partner?** If you dream about getting your product into the hands of people on every continent and your partner would rather focus on one area, conflicts will arise.

✔ **Does your personality match or compliment your potential partner's?** Depending on how you work, you may want someone who is very similar to you or very different. Do you prefer someone who will challenge you often and bring a whole new perspective? Or do you like the smooth sailing of someone whose work style matches yours?

✔ **Is your potential partner reliable?** Be sure you know your would-be partner's business history inside-out before entering into a contract.

Succeeding in a foreign market takes long-term commitment. Be sure that your partner is as willing and able to stick with it as you.

Managing Your Goods Through an Intermediary

You may be leaning pretty strongly toward direct exporting, and that's fine if you know you're up to it. But even if you're a lone wolf or just really like to do it yourself, don't rule out going through an intermediary just yet; read the next sections before you personally take that 12-hour overseas flight to start selling.

Pros and cons of going through an intermediary

Besides the good or service that your business is exporting, what's your most precious commodity? Your *time*, of course! That's where an intermediary can be of great value to you, because they can save you tons of it.

Consider some of the advantages:

- ✔ Your intermediary helps you enter the foreign market more quickly.

- ✔ Your customers may feel more comfortable dealing with your intermediary, especially at first.

However, consider the disadvantages to using an intermediary as well:

- ✔ You have to pay the intermediary, so you don't make as high a return on your exporting investment.

- ✔ You may have to set your prices a bit higher to compensate for what you pay the intermediary and, therefore, your prices may not be as competitive as you'd like.

When you're considering an intermediary, perform all the necessary due diligence. Choosing the wrong intermediary (unqualified, untrustworthy, or just plain no good) will seriously hurt your business. (For some tips, see "What to consider when choosing an intermediary" later in this chapter.)

Types of intermediaries

Three main types of intermediaries exist. This section looks at the characteristics of each to help you decide which (if any) is best for your business.

Agents and representatives

You may authorize either type to enter into contracts or sales agreements on your behalf, but agents and representatives aren't exactly the same.

- ✔ An *agent* secures foreign orders from foreign customers, and in exchange, you pay him or her a commission.

- ✔ A *representative* is similar to an agent but more specialized. This person works within a specific geographic area, sells related lines of goods or services, and is also paid by commission.

You benefit from using a good foreign agent or representative in many ways. They perform a wide range of tasks for you:

- ✔ Advising on financing and transportation
- ✔ Clearing customs
- ✔ Collecting money
- ✔ Getting access to local customers
- ✔ Researching markets
- ✔ Supplying you with information about local business practices, laws, and cultural traditions

Using a foreign agent or representative gives you immediate presence in your target market, which is cheaper than setting up base yourself. The agent or representative can probably make more sales calls than you could, which could increase your sales more quickly.

Foreign distributors

A foreign distributor buys your product or service from you and resells it locally. With this type of intermediary you can gain *after-sales services* (services that take place after the customer buys the product, such as repairs or troubleshooting help) in a foreign market. Foreign distributors usually:

> ✔ Guarantee warranties and repairs
>
> ✔ Offer financing to buyers
>
> ✔ Set the selling price

Using a foreign distributor could reduce your profits, not only because you have to pay them, but also because they set the local selling price. You may have less control over your product and its price, which might not work for you if you're used to having a lot of control in your business.

Trading houses

A *trading house* in an intermediary located in Canada that markets your goods or services overseas. Some trading houses are principal or export merchants who buy products directly from Canadian suppliers; others act as agents that sell products on commission. A trading house might specialize in a certain industry or a certain foreign market.

If a trading house is full service, it can handle many tasks for you, such as:

> ✔ Arranging transportation
>
> ✔ Doing market research
>
> ✔ Exhibiting at trade shows
>
> ✔ Filling out required documentation
>
> ✔ Hiring distributors
>
> ✔ Preparing advertising

You may be thinking of using a trading house to get into your target market. When you're choosing one, keep the following elements in mind:

> ✔ **The trading house's areas of specialty:** If you export nail polish and the trading house is experienced with fruit juice, you may need a better match.
>
> ✔ **The trading house's strongest services:** Might the clock radios you're exporting require repairs after they've sold (see our definition of after-sales services in the previous section)? Then a trading house with special connections with electronic repair services in your target market would be a great fit.

> ✔ **The trading house's market expertise:** Some trading houses are very knowledgeable about South Africa, while others deal with Australia almost exclusively. You want the trading house's market focus to be the same as yours.

See the web site for the Canadian Federation of Trading House Associations (www.caftha.ca) for more information on finding a trading house that works for your export business.

What to consider when choosing an intermediary

Starting by word of mouth is always a good idea when you're looking to hire an intermediary. Ask exporting colleagues whom they recommend, and speak with potential customers to find out if they've had any particularly good (or bad) experiences with specific intermediaries. You can also get information through Canadian Trade Commissioners abroad, trade associations, business councils, and banks.

You'll likely come across several potential intermediaries. Make a shortlist of the best ones and proceed just as you would when hiring an employee: Meet with the intermediary and always check references.

If you have a good feeling about an intermediary, but you're not ready to enter into a long-term agreement, you can agree to work together for a trial period. That way, if the experience is not what you expected or the intermediary is not a good match for your business, you can dissolve the relationship once the trial period is over.

You'll need to take a number of considerations into account when choosing an intermediary. The following questions can help you make a choice that will work well for your exporting venture:

> ✔ **How big is your sales force?** Find out how many salespeople they actually have and whether that number suits your needs. If the number is small, is the intermediary capable and willing to expand its sales force for your business?
>
> ✔ **What territories do you cover?** Find out if it covers the areas you want to enter, and if it has offices and

representatives in those territories. Does the intermediary plan to expand into other markets in the future?

✔ **What is your sales record?** Find out if the intermediary's sales are generally consistent. Try to figure out its sales volume for the past five years.

✔ **May I speak with other exporters that you represent?** Talking with others and checking references is always a good way to gauge if the intermediary is reliable.

✔ **May I see your equipment and facilities?** Find out if it has a big enough warehouse to accommodate your products and how it controls stock levels. Verify that its computer system works with yours. If your products need repairs, could the intermediary do them or be trained to do them?

✔ **What products or services are your specialties?** Enquire about the products or services it represents and see if they're compatible with yours — your line of specialty cocktail glasses may not go well with their glow-in-the-dark Beethoven busts, for example. Ask if it has worked with Canadian products before and check for any possible conflicts of interest.

✔ **How would you promote my product or service?** Find out how it promotes sales, through what type of media, and if it has an adequate advertising budget. How many names are on its direct mail mailing list and are these prospects compatible with your business? Ask if the intermediary has a web site and be sure to check it out.

✔ **What are your internal policies on sales staff?** Find out how its sales staff is compensated (such as through salaries, incentives, or motivational programs) and how it monitors sales staff's performance. Ask if sales staff receive training and how the training works. See if the intermediary would be willing to share the cost of sending staff to seminars.

✔ **Who are your customers?** Get a sense of its customer profile and see if the customers' interests are compatible with your product or service. Do they have a few big accounts or many small accounts, and where does the bulk of their revenue come from?

✔ **How many exporters do you represent?** Determine if you would be a primary supplier or just one of many. Get a sense of how much of the intermediary's business you would represent and how you compare to its other principals.

A great tool for finding potential intermediaries is TRACE, a non-profit association of multinational companies and intermediaries. They specialize in anti-bribery due diligence reviews, and compliance training for sales agents, representatives, consultants, distributors, and suppliers. Member companies can access the TRACE intermediary list of members who fulfill strict due diligence reviews. See www.traceinternational.org for more information.

Shipping Your Goods

So everything is in shape. Now you want to start shipping those goods! Of course, shipping isn't as simple as tossing your product in a box with some bubble wrap and sending it out into the big wide world. This section goes over some of the procedures exporters need to follow when moving products.

Knowing the rules

The Canadian government regulates trade and customs activities pretty heavily, and most other countries do the same. So not only do you have to familiarize yourself with domestic export laws, but you also have to learn those of the country to which you're exporting. Obeying all of these regulations to the T is important and requires some work on your part. For example, if you're exporting a service, you may need to get professionally accredited in another country, even if you already are in Canada. Visit Foreign Affairs and International Trade Canada's Web site at www.international.gc.ca for more information about export controls and regulations.

Getting export permits and declarations

Two types of permits exist in Canada: a General Export Permit and an Individual Export Permit. But how do you know if you need one?

If you're exporting to a country that's on the *Area Control List* (a list of countries that require exporters to have permits, except for humanitarian items), then you have to get a permit.

You may also need a permit when the goods you're exporting are on the *Export Control List*. This is a list of goods and technologies that, under the Export and Import Permits Act, require export permits reported from Canada.

To find out more about export and import permits and controls, go to the Web site of Foreign Affairs and International Trade Canada at www.international.gc.ca.

You may also need an *export declaration*, which provides details of what you're shipping, such as contents, value, and destination. One example is the CBSA B13A Export Declaration, which is a mandatory form that exporters must prepare for every country excluding the U.S.

The Canada Border Services Agency (CBSA) can help you determine which declarations you may need. On their Web site (www.cbsa.gc.ca) check under the Forms and Publications Search for the document RC4116, *Exporting Goods from Canada*.

Having the right documentation

Paper, paper everywhere! The exporting business requires that many documents be completed, and just thinking about it is enough to make you consider staying in your warm domestic nest. But not so fast! You don't have to deal with all this paperwork yourself. That's what freight forwarders and customs brokers are for. What are they? Read on...

Customs broker

A *customs broker* takes care of all those tricky bits, such as clearing goods through customs, preparing customs documentation, and paying duties on exported goods. Plus, a customs broker can help you stay up-to-date with recent information about tariff changes or new developments in customs regulations. A customs broker's fees depend on what you're exporting, where you're exporting it, and the amounts you're exporting.

The Canadian Society of Customs Brokers (CSCB) is the professional society for customs brokers in Canada. See their Web site for information about hiring a customs broker and their membership directory (www.cscb.ca).

Freight forwarder

Freight forwarders are agencies that can handle all your exporting logistical requirements, such as negotiating rates with shipping lines, airlines, trucking companies, customs brokers, and insurance firms. They can also help you clarify transaction conditions if you're using letters of credit (see Chapter 5). Here's a simplified breakdown of what the freight forwarder does:

1. Your freight forwarder sends the goods to the carrier.

2. Your customer receives all the necessary documents, which allow the shipment to clear customs.

3. The goods clear customs at their port of entry.

Freight forwarders may specialize in certain countries or in a particular type of good. Using a freight forwarder cuts back your delivery times and improves customer service.

Find listings for freight forwarders in Canada at Freightnet, which has over 21,000 international members (www.freighnet.com). They provide you with a free sample quote when you complete an online form. Also check out the Canadian International Freight Forwarders' Association (CIFFA). It is a professional association that represents both freight forwarders and associate members such as port authorities, law firms, and insurance companies. You can search their list of members by region to contact freight forwarders to work with your export business (www.ciffa.com).

On the Road: Delivering Your Goods

Goods won't deliver themselves, unfortunately, so you must decide on the best way to get them from point A (where they're made) to point B (the customer).

You want your product to arrive safe and sound for the right price. Although many exporters would love to hire a concord jet for every delivery, that probably isn't in your budget, so factor in the cost when choosing a delivery method.

Four main methods of delivery exist, and you may opt to use one or a combination of two or more to get the goods to their destination.

You can choose to ship by air (which is quick but pricey) or sea carrier (slow and cheap) to move your goods overseas, then decide how they will reach their final destination. The options for ground shipping—train or truck—are the same internationally as when moving goods across North America, although the trucking business may not be reliable in some non-industrialized countries.

Packing up your goods

Most people have had the experience of a long-awaited package arriving, only to find that its contents are damaged beyond repair. What a shame. You definitely want your goods to arrive at their destination in one piece (unless you export puzzles).

Keep your goods safe and sound by following these tips:

✔ **Anticipate the worst.** Assume your goods will take the road less traveled (and possibly unpaved). Package them to withstand getting jostled, dropped, and wet, cold, hot, or both, depending on your chosen mode of transport.

✔ **Trust (almost) no one.** If the packaging is flimsy, anyone can easily open it and steal your goods. Solid packaging that takes some effort to get into is best.

Visit the Virtual Canadian Trade Commissioner Service site (`infoexport.gc.ca.`) for packaging tips and advice.

Insuring your goods

You can never be too careful, right? You've packaged your shipment properly—now, buy cargo insurance (usually costs one to two percent of the goods' value, and worth the peace of mind).

The type of insurance you need depends on how you're shipping your goods. For example, many railway carriers fully compensate you for lost or damaged goods, while other carriers only cover an agreed amount.

Your freight forwarder or customs broker (which we discuss earlier in this chapter) may offer insurance services.

Labelling and marking your goods properly

You don't want your goods to get lost because no one can identify them. Proper labelling — with more than a destination and return address — is key.

In some cases, labelling, advertising, or packaging restrictions may apply to your goods (for example, label requirements for product weight of electrical standards). Your goods could get stuck at customs if you ignore these standards, causing lost profits, wasted time, and headaches for you.

Markings on containers set your good apart from other shippers' products, correspond with the commercial invoice or bill of lading, and include some or all of the following:

✔ Buyer's name, address, and telephone number

✔ Country of origin, such as "Made in Canada"

✔ Handling instructions (may include warnings)

✔ Package dimensions, such as width, height, and weight

✔ Packing list that tells the number of and contents of each package in the shipment (each container includes one copy)

✔ Port of entry at the importing country.

Chapter 7

Exporting to the U.S.

● ●

In This Chapter

▶ Thinking about the U.S. market

▶ Looking at NAFTA

▶ Dealing with barriers to the U.S. market

▶ Discovering sources for researching the U.S. market

● ●

*Y*ou've got the whole world to think about as a potential export market, but how far do you really have to go? You've likely considered our southern neighbour, the United States, as a logical choice. This chapter offers information on details — trade agreements and market research sources, for example — specific to the United States.

Considering Exporting to the U.S.

The United States can evoke feelings of love and hate, desire to conquer, and fear of being conquered in an exporter. You have a lot to consider, so we start with the some of the reasons your export business should head south:

✔ **Proximity to Canada:** Because the United States is right next door, your goods may not have as far to go as they would if you were shipping them overseas. Your travel time for business trips could be shorter, too.

✔ **Cultural similarities:** Although the United States and Canada are very different countries, we do share many characteristics, including a language, standards of living, and consumer attitudes.

✔ **Sheer size:** The U.S. is the world's largest economic power and has a population that is about ten times the size of Canada's — approximately 291 million people. That's a lot of potential customers!

Exporting to the land of opportunity has some downsides. Keep these points in mind as you plan exporting south:

✔ **False sense of security:** The qualities that draw our countries together can also fool Canadian exporters into feeling too comfortable. You can't know everything about the U.S. just by watching American TV. To successfully enter any marketplace, you must be sensitive and pay attention to what makes it distinct.

Pay attention to all of the details of the market — or rather markets (we talk more about markets in Chapter 2). The U.S. marketplace comprises many diverse segments and as long as you're exporting a strong product with a solid plan behind it, you have the same opportunity for success as the thousands of other companies who succeeded in the U.S.

✔ **Incredibly competitive conditions:** The United States is huge and does a lot of business. Even if your business is a fairly major player domestically, you may be the smallest fish in the pond when you cross the border.

✔ **Complex border issues:** With a heightened awareness of global terrorism, you can't just waltz across the border and start selling. Security and tariff issues (which we discuss later in this chapter) are serious matters and if you don't follow the rules, your goods won't get far.

Exporting Legalese

Although you're certainly not expected to know each and every American business law by heart, knowing as much as you can helps you to plan your American export venture. Have at least a working knowledge of a few of the major legal issues and agreements between Canada and the United States. In this section, we briefly look at NAFTA rules, U.S. tax laws, and Canadian customs and export regulations. More information on those topics is available in the online publication *U.S. Regulations for Canadian Exporters* at www.cbsc.org/alberta/content/us_reg.pdf. It makes for a handy quick reference when your lawyer is out for lunch!

Understanding NAFTA

The North American Free Trade Agreement has been both a source of pleasure and frustration to Canadians since its inception in 1994, but we recommend that you try to wrap your head around it as you enter the U.S. market. In essence, NAFTA was designed to remove trade and investment impediments between the United States, Canada, and Mexico. The basis of this agreement is pretty simple, but its details — especially when it comes to the exporting business — are quite complex.

You can find background on the NAFTA agreement on the Foreign Affairs and International Trade Canada Web site at www.international.gc.ca/nafta-alena/menu-en.asp.

NAFTA affects two main areas of your export venture:

- ✔ **NAFTA Rules of Origin:** Products that are made in the NAFTA countries get *preferential tariff treatment* (the duty rates are lower) when they pass between Canada, the U.S., and Mexico. The rules vary depending upon the product.

  When you export goods to the U.S., you need to fill out a *certificate of origin* to accompany your shipment. Certificates of origin are documents that show the products' country of origin, so the products get preferential tariff treatment.

  To find out if your goods qualify under the rules of origin, visit Foreign Affairs and International Trade Canada's Web site.

- ✔ **Businesspeople crossing the border:** NAFTA lets some businesspeople cross the border for work through temporary work visas. Visas are useful if, say, you want to set up base with Canadian employees in the United States. However, the criteria for getting a work visa are quite specific, so look at the labour list quite thoroughly before assuming that this route will work for you.

U.S. tax laws

We have one recommendation for you: hire a professional. Having an accountant or lawyer who specializes in U.S. tax law for exporters is invaluable if you're exporting to the US. Just like in Canada and in every other country, tax laws in the United States are complex. You may have to deal with federal taxes, state taxes, and local taxes. When you're trying to make money, as you are in your export business, you want to explore all of the tax avenues that can help you out (and know how to avoid those that might hurt you, too). Talk to your current accountant and colleagues to get a referral to an accountant who specializes in U.S. tax law.

Essentially, as an exporter you want to avoid *double taxation* (getting taxed both in the Canada and the United States). The Canadian and U.S. governments set up the Canada-United States Tax Treaty for this purpose. The Treaty regulates which country gets to collect taxes from people and businesses that live or operate in both countries.

However, avoiding double taxation can be difficult. Individual American states don't have to follow the Canada-United States Tax Treaty. That means that the state in which you're doing business can tax the income that your business earns, even if you're already paying income tax in your home province. An accountant or lawyer who specializes in U.S. tax law is your best source of advice on navigating the tax systems.

Here are a few good sources for information about U.S. tax laws:

✔ The Internal Revenue Service (IRS): www.irs.gov

✔ Taxsites.com (federal, state, and local taxes): www.taxsites.com

✔ Multistate Tax Commission, which includes links to all state tax departments: www.mtc.gov

Customs and exporting regulations

If you're exporting to the U.S. and your goods aren't manufactured in Canada, you want to avoid any legal or regulatory issues when you import goods into the United States.

The Office of Foreign Assets Control (OFAC) Web site currently identifies five countries that have trade sanctions against them which include: Cuba, Iran, Myanmar (formerly Burma), North Korea, and Sudan.

As you might expect from a basic knowledge of American history, you cannot import cigars from Cuba and export them to the United States. In fact, importing any Cuban good or service into the U.S. is prohibited under the Cuban Liberty and Democratic Solidarity (Libertad) Act of 1996.

You can contact the Canadian Embassy in Washington or check out the Office of Foreign Assets Control Web site for more information on sanctions at `www.treas.gov/offices/enforcement/ofac`.

Looking at the U.S. Market

The U.S. marketplace is created not from one singular, united identity as you may find in other more homogeneous countries, but of many small markets. Each market is created from a diverse group of characteristics that comprise the United States itself, including age, ethnic background, gender, level of income, occupation, political beliefs, and religious beliefs.

Unlike in Canada, where the differences between residents of different provinces exist but are reconcilable (for the most part), people from one part of the States often have very different tastes than those from another.

Exporting to the States isn't as simple as spreading your goods all across the country. You need to research territories — the North versus the South, the East versus the West or versus the interior — to know in which territory your product is most likely to succeed.

In this section, we discuss a few sources you can use to research U.S. markets.

Researching statistics on U.S. markets

Before you start shipping (we talk more about that in Chapter 6), you need to determine where your product or service will fit best in the U.S. Where will it be in the highest demand?

One way to determine where your product will sell best is to check out the previous U.S. demand for products that are similar to yours. If you know what has been imported into various markets in the U.S., you can see if your product has a place.

A good starting point is the Trade Data Online tools on Industry Canada's Strategis Web site (www.strategis.ic.gc.ca/ sc_mrkti/tdst/engdoc/tr_homep.html). Using data from Statistics Canada and the U.S. Census Bureau, it provides you with statistics on the types and quantities of goods traded between Canada and the U.S. The stats help you find out what U.S. markets might have demand for your goods and might even point you to U.S. markets you haven't yet considered.

Another source to research U.S. markets is the Bureau of Economic Analysis (BEA) at www.bea.gov. The BEA is an agent of the U.S. Department of Commerce and is all about the numbers. The BEA provides economic data (statistics) about the U.S. to show how their economy is doing. You can find stats for economic activity by region — state residents' personal income and average corporate profits by industry — and stats on *gross domestic products* (GDP, which is the total value of goods that the U.S. produces). Use this information to get an accurate economic picture of your target U.S. market. That way, you won't end up exporting designer stiletto shoes to a market with a low average income and slow economy.

Discovering more about U.S. markets

Many other organizations provide stats and information to give exporters a clear picture of U.S. markets. Try the following Web sites for market reports, fact sheets, profiles, and hard numbers:

- ✔ **Canada-United States Relations Web site of Foreign Affairs and International Trade Canada** (http://geo. international.gc.ca/can-am/main/menu-en.asp): The site's "Trade and Investment" section provides information about trade and business by specific region or by specific industry. It also offers fact sheets about trade for 38 states.

- ✔ **Canadian Trade Commissioner Service** (infoexport. gc.ca): This site contains information about specific regional U.S. markets, such as economic profiles and fact sheets about Canada–U.S. exports, to help you assess your product's potential.

- ✔ **FedBizOpps** (www.fedbizopps.gov): This site is a portal to federal business opportunities where sellers can post their products and services. It describes how the U.S. government buys products and services.

- ✔ **Stat-USA/Internet** (www.stat-usa.gov): This site is a database of information about specific areas of the U.S. economy (retail prices, financial trends, and gross domestic product, for example). Subscriptions cost $200 for one year or $75 for three months.

- ✔ **U.S. Census Bureau** (www.census.gov): This site is a leading source for data about the population and economy of the U.S.

Barriers to the U.S. Market

Earlier in this chapter, we discuss how entering the U.S. market isn't as simple as you might think, despite our neighbourly relationship. Agreements such as NAFTA are in place to help trade between Canada and the U.S. (and Mexico), but a great number of barriers still exist. In this section, we talk about some of the barriers that you might face, such as tariffs and security issues.

To find out more about the political and cultural barriers to the U.S. market, check out Foreign Affairs Canada's Canada–United States Relations Web site at www.can-am.gc.ca. The site gives you a useful and frequently updated overview of current trade issues between Canada and the U.S.

Emergency barriers

Sometimes the United States closes its borders to certain goods when major events occur. The U.S. and Canada are each other's biggest trading partners, and the Canadian export industry relies heavily on selling goods to the U.S. If you export a good deemed restricted by the U.S. government (even if it's only restricted for a short time) your business will suffer.

An example of this kind of emergency barrier is the Mad Cow Disease scare of 2003. The United States (and countries around the world) put a ban on Canadian exported beef after a cow was diagnosed with the disease in Alberta. Beef exports are big business in Canada (this country was the world's third biggest beef exporter). Just three months after the ban, Canadian beef export values fell to almost nothing. The Canadian agricultural industry, and particularly beef farmers, took a huge hit and lost over $1 billion.

In this extreme case, the Canadian government offered financing to businesses that the ban affected, however, you can't run your export business on government support alone. You can voice your concerns about export bans to Foreign Affairs and International Trade Canada.

Tariffs

A *tariff* is a tax on imported or exported goods. The amount of a tariff may be set based on a percentage of the value of the goods or a set rate.

A government may charge a tariff as a way to make money. Another reason to charge a tariff on an imported good is to keep similar domestic products competitive with the imported ones — basically, to prevent exporters from selling their goods at prices so low that domestic businesses can't compete. If exporters have to pay tariffs on products as they cross the border, they'll have to make up for that cost by selling the products at a higher price.

NAFTA has practically eliminated all tariffs on goods passing between North American countries. Check with Foreign Affairs and International Trade Canada to be sure that no tariffs apply to your goods.

Non-tariff barriers

Removing tariffs was supposed to make trade between Canada and the U.S. fair. But governments can enact policies that tip the odds in their favour, which are called *non-tariff barriers* (NTBs) — basically any trade barrier than isn't a tariff. Generally, NTBs hurt trade, and exporters and many governments consider them unfair trading practice. Here are some examples of NTBs:

- ✔ **Import quotas:** The government limits the number of a certain good that can enter the country.

- ✔ **Specific manufacturing or production conditions:** The government insists that an imported product must be made according to its own standards. If the product isn't, it can't be imported.

- ✔ **Intellectual property issues:** A government claims a certain product violates its intellectual property laws and bans the product from being imported. (See Chapter 10 for more about intellectual property.)

- ✔ **Technical barriers:** The importing government requires extra testing or certification of a good.

Protect yourself against the economic effects of an unexpected NTB by doing your research in advance. If a barrier does exist, ask yourself the following questions to determine whether or not you should press on with your U.S. export venture under a particular product or service:

- ✔ How does the barrier affect my access to the U.S. market?

- ✔ How does the barrier affect the pricing of my product or service?

- ✔ How does the barrier affect the ultimate cost of doing business in the United States?

- ✔ Is it worth the financial implications?

For the most part, exporters' goods travel across the Canada-U.S. border without any problems (over $1 billion worth of goods per day, in fact!). But hey, stuff happens. Sometimes NTBs do arise, but only very rarely (see the sidebar "The hard facts on softwood" for a well-known example).

But if a barrier does arise in Canada–U.S. trade issues, don't throw in the towel on your exporting venture — all is not lost! These difficulties can be resolved in a few different ways:

- ✔ **Discussion:** Government officials from the U.S. and Canada consult with each other to find a common ground and get rid of the barrier.

- ✔ **World Trade Organization (WTO):** The country can appeal to the WTO dispute settlement panel and present its case. WTO decisions are non-binding, however.

- ✔ **NAFTA:** A country can appeal to NAFTA's dispute settlement panel. The decision is binding.

Foreign Affairs and International Trade Canada is the government department to contact if you're facing an NTB. You can make a request to them to help resolve your dispute.

The hard facts of softwood

Ever had a disagreement with your neighbour, perhaps over that tree you're both sure is on each other's property? Well, the softwood lumber dispute between Canada and the United States is anything but neighbourly. It's one of the longest-running trade disputes in North American history.

In Canada, provincial and federal governments set lumber prices. In the U.S., prices are set competitively. The United States claimed that the Canadian federal and provincial governments unfairly subsidized their lumber industry, keeping the prices of softwood lumber much lower here than in the U.S.

In 1986, the U.S. Department of Commerce (DOC) imposed a 15 percent tariff on softwood exported from Canada. The countries negotiated a Memorandum of Understanding (MOU) that Canada would collect a 15 percent tax on softwood exports to replace the tariff. But the MOU was heavily criticized by the Canadian government and it was terminated in the early 1990s. The DOC then charged a 6.5 percent duty tax on Canadian softwood.

Canada appealed to the Free Trade Agreement (FTA, which is NAFTA today) panel. The panel ruled that the U.S. had to return the $1 billion in duties it had collected on Canadian softwood. In 1996, both countries implemented the five-year Softwood Lumber Agreement (SLA), which let a limited amount of softwood be exported to the U.S. tax-free. When the SLA expired, the U.S. filed two petitions against Canada (for subsidizing the lumber industry and dumping low-cost wood in the U.S). Canada appealed the petitions under the WTO (which settled in Canada's favour) and a NAFTA panel (which also settled in favour of Canada in 2004).

On October 12, 2006, Canada and the U.S. put into practice the 2006 Softwood Lumber Agreement. The 2006 SLA cancelled all U.S. countervailing and anti-dumping taxes, and will have the U.S. return the nearly $5 billion in duties it collected from Canadian softwood producers.

Security

If you've taken a plane to the U.S. since September 11, 2001, you're definitely aware of how significantly security issues have affected border traffic. You may have experienced the scrutiny and long lineups at customs when you cross the border. Well, any goods you export have to go through the same sort of process. Increased border security means that your exports might face delays in transit.

A slew of regulations, programs, and policies put into place since the events of 9/11 affect the daily movement of goods into (and out of) the United States. The Smart Border Declaration and Action Plan, signed by Canada and the United States, details 32 initiatives to help both countries cooperate in border and security management.

Canada–U.S. border risk-management programs

Canada Border Services Agency (CBSA) works with the United States government to create programs for keeping trade safe, even in times of possible risk. Here are some programs exporters should be aware of:

- ✔ **Customs–Trade Partnership against Terrorism (C–TPAT):** C–TPAT is a program that encourages Canadian exporting companies to enhance their security programs. It is a voluntary program in which the U.S. Customs and Border Protection designates certain Canadian companies as low-risk. The goods of these companies can pass through the border more quickly.

  To qualify for C–TPAT, your company may need to upgrade property and personnel security procedures, which costs money. Export Development Canada offers a security-compliance loan to finance companies that are enhancing their security standards. Visit www.edc.ca/ctpat/support for more information on C–TPAT.

- ✔ **The Free and Secure Trade (FAST) program:** A joint Canada–U.S. program with the CBSA, Citizenship and Immigration Canada, and U.S. Customs and Border

Protection. Members of FAST have their goods cleared through an expedited process. The program is available at major border crossings, and importers, drivers, and carriers are eligible.

✔ **The Partners in Protection (PIP) program:** A goodwill arrangement between private-sector businesses and the CBSA to increase border security and prevent smuggling into the U.S. Your business provides the CBSA with a self-assessment of your security methods and in return the CBSA helps you fix any security flaws.

To keep track of risk-management programs between Canada and the United States, as well as wait times for goods at major border crossings, visit the CBSA's Web site.

U.S. regulations affecting exporters

Some regulations in the U.S. could affect your exporting venture. Here are a few to be aware of:

✔ *The Bioterrorism Act:* Under this act, Canadian businesses that export food or feed to the United States are required to keep careful records. These records basically trace the food's journey, showing where it started and where it's heading. They also state the number of packages in the shipment and a description of the shipment. If you plan to export food, contact Agriculture and Agri-Food Canada (ats.agr.ca) about how you can comply with these rules.

✔ *The Trade Act of 2002:* If you're trading with the United States, you need to provide advance notice of the arrival of goods at the U.S. border. How much notice you're required to give depends on whether your business is registered with the FAST program, which we discuss earlier in this chapter.

"Buy-American" Rules

The United States government requires some organizations (usually federal government organizations) to buy only American goods whenever possible. This means that Canadian exports may take a back seat to domestically produced products in a lot of large markets.

Even though many federal U.S. agencies have "Buy-American" policies, you might be able to crack those markets with the help of the Canadian Commercial Corporation (CCC). The CCC offers two programs for Canadian exporters to compete with American companies who must buy U.S. goods:

✔ **General Services Administration (GSA) Schedules Program submission service**: If your business is approved and on the GSA schedule, you can compete with American companies and bid to sell the GSA your products or services. The CCC helps you complete your application and advises you on contracts.

✔ **Department of Defense prime contractor solution:** This program helps Canadian exporters register their products or services to sell to the U.S. Department of Defense. The CCC acts as the contractor to negotiate favourable terms and payment guarantees.

Visit www.ccc.ca for information about these programs.

Additional sources for researching the U.S. market

You probably still have a lot of questions about the U.S. market, particularly when it comes to how it can work with your exporting business. These online sources help you go beyond the information in this chapter.

✔ **Canadian Commercial Corporation** (www.ccc.ca)

✔ **EuroMonitor International:** An online source for reference books about the U.S. market and economy. (www.euromonitor.com)

✔ **Europa World Book:** Online reference books of economic and political information (www.europaworld.com)

✔ **Export Development Canada** (www.edc.ca)

✔ **Foreign Affairs and International Trade Canada** (international.gc.ca)

✔ **Team Canada Inc (TCI):** (exportsource.ca)

Training Programs

If you'd still like an added sense of security after conducting all of this market research, you can try a training program. ExportUSA offers training sessions for becoming an exporter to the United States. They last from one to three days and are often centred around a trade show, so you can get information related to your specific industry. For a participation fee of $100 U.S., you learn about border procedures and relevant U.S. markets. Also, you meet with Canadian Trade Officers, agents, and distributors. Check out the ExportUSA Web site at www.infoexport.gc.ca/en/DisplayDocument.jsp?did=5272 for more information.

Here are the three programs ExportUSA offers:

- **Reverse NEBS (New Exporters to Border States):** All you need to qualify for this program is to be a Canadian company with an interest in exporting to the United States. ExportUSA holds these seminars in cities across Canada, which focus on a specific export sector.

- **NEBS:** This program is designed for companies that are incorporated, operate in Canada, and are interested in exporting to the U.S. NEBS introduces you to the essentials of exporting. The focus is on export education and Canadian companies are the target audience, which means you will find practical and relevant information.

- **Exporters to the United States (EXTUS):** This is the program for you if your business is already exporting to the U.S. and your U.S. sales are less than $2.3 million. If you're interested in expanding your current export venture to other regions of the U.S., EXTUS shows you how to break into new markets and helps with networking.

You can also try the Forum for International Trade Training (FITT) at www.fitt.ca, an organization that concentrates on expanding the skills of Canadian exporters so that they can compete in world markets.

Chapter 8

E-Exporting

*T*he 21st century is an exciting time to be in business, and it's an especially exciting time for exporters. Technology makes going global easier, faster, and cheaper than ever. You want to consider taking advantage of everything that technology has to offer your exporting business.

This chapter assumes that you already have some kind of Web presence and looks at ways that you can make e-business solutions work for you.

If, however, you aren't online yet, getting a Web site is easier and cheaper than you think. Speak to colleagues or other business owners about Internet service providers (ISPs) and Web hosting services. They can help you build a Web site for your business and even find the resources to manage it for you.

Decoding E-Business

In the age of all things electronic, you see that little letter "e" stuck in front of a lot of words. Well, the concept of e-business can have a strong impact on your exporting venture if you know what it means and how to take advantage of it.

Basically, e-*business* is doing business over the Internet, including buying and selling goods and services, providing customer support, and dealing with business partners. You may be doing some of these activities already.

E-business and e-commerce aren't synonymous, though they sound very similar. *E-commerce* is the term that describes online financial transactions.

Considering the benefits of e-business

The Internet is a great tool that can help you in all areas of your exporting venture. Of course, the time you save is probably the biggest benefit to e-business, and conducting e-business helps you save time in many of your everyday business activities. E-business gives you

- ✔ Fast access to international markets
- ✔ Flexible and adaptable marketing and advertising online
- ✔ More efficient customer service
- ✔ Nearly instant delivery of documents over e-mail, rather than waiting for real-time delivery
- ✔ Simple, efficient ordering systems

Naturally, conducting business electronically can't eliminate the good old-fashioned legwork involved in exporting, such as shipping, customs regulations, and work permits. What e-business does is make it quicker and easier for you to communicate with customers and partners and to connect to your international markets.

No special set of regulations exists for conducting export business over the Internet. The same rules apply whether you're conducting e-business or doing business in a more traditional way.

Deciding if you can do export e-business

To compete with other companies in ever expanding cyber-space, sit down take a look at your export business. Does it have e-business potential? If so, how big is its potential? Considering these factors in terms of how your business uses the Internet helps you find the answers:

- ✔ **Your current Web site:** How do you use your Web site? What information does your Web site provide customers? What information does your Web site provide to you?

- ✔ **Your customer service:** How efficient is your customer service? Do you offer customized support?

- ✔ **Your customers:** Do they use the Internet? Might they use it to buy from your business or from your competition?

- ✔ **Your online customer relationships:** Do your customers use the Internet to interact with your business? Do you find new customers through the Internet? How do you get customer feedback?

- ✔ **Your online usage:** Do you order supplies or services for your business online?

- ✔ **Your operations:** Are your operating policies and proce-dures on record electronically? Does your business have an Intranet (an internal Web site for staff)? Can your business support integrated customer service and quick expansion?

If you find your answers lean strongly toward using the Internet for your business, your company's definitely got what it takes to success in e-business.

If you're still not sure whether or not e-business is right for your export business, Industry Canada's ebiz.enable Diagnostic Tools (at www.cipo.gc.ca/ebizenable) can help. You can use the tools to determine whether e-business is relevant to your export venture and if your current business is ready to launch into cyberspace.

Looking at Your Web Site

If you're on top of things, you most likely look at your business's Web site every day. But this time, take a good, in-depth look at it. As a businessperson, you probably want your Web site to work for you in a number of ways, such as the following. Is your Web site

- ✔ An excellent source of information for your customers about your products or services?

- ✔ Completely safe and secure so your customers can order from you and pay you with confidence?

- ✔ Easy for customers to navigate and find their profiles and histories?

- ✔ Reliable, so your customers can count on it when they need to?

- ✔ Aesthetically appealing to your customers?

If your Web site accomplishes all of these things, then it's probably doing a good job of meeting your domestic clients' needs. Great, because expanding and modifying your web site to suit an international market is easier with a solid foundation. However, after thinking about the questions, you may find that your Web site falls a bit short. In that case, consider improving your existing site before preparing your exporting e-business. You may even hire professional Web designers and writers to get your site up to snuff.

An important difference exists between an export business's Web site and a domestic business's site. Because your target market might be overseas, you need to *localize* or adapt your site for that market. The elements of localization include

- ✔ **Language:** Have your Web site translated into the native language of your target market.

    Only use professional translators who are familiar with your target market. If you hire your cousin because he got an A in high school French, the results could be disastrous.

- ✔ **Branding:** Make it reflect the target market's culture, traditions, and laws.

✔ **Currency denomination:** Although paying in U.S. dollars is common, some customers may insist on paying you in their own currency.

Getting technical

If you're a small- to medium-size business and you or your staff run your business's Web site in-house, you might consider outsourcing it to a larger company. Find a company that's well equipped to handle the heavier technical requirements — and very importantly, security issues — of Internet-based exporting. If, however, you're managing your Web site yourself, be sure your e-business system has the following components:

✔ **Backup system for your data:** Anything can happen, so be prepared. Have a plan to back up your important data either daily or weekly, using a second hard drive, for example.

✔ **Data encryption:** Sensitive information, such as passwords or bank account numbers, is scrambled so only those who are intended to read it can do so.

✔ **Digital certificates:** These certificates authenticate online transactions, e-mails, and your server, to be sure that only intended users can view information.

✔ **Firewalls for hardware and software:** A set of programs that keeps outside users from accessing your network.

✔ **Office security:** Keep your office doors locked when no one is around, so outsiders can't access your computer system.

✔ **Internet safety use:** Not all Web sites are safe and some even contain viruses that can damage your computer system. Only visit sites you can trust and never opened attachments unless you know who sent them.

✔ **Secure Sockets Layer (SSL):** This technology lets you transmit data securely from your Web site to a customer's Web browser.

✔ **Updated software:** When software has been available for a while, hackers have usually figured out how to exploit its loopholes. So keep your computer software up-to-date at all times. Your software will usually prompt you to download updates over the Internet.

Discuss these elements with your Web hosting service to keep your business's information, your customers' information, and your Web site's contents secure.

E-Customers

As a new exporter, you're expanding your business. You know that your customers are out there, somewhere, in the big wide world. The question is, how do you find them? Not being able to see or shake hands with your e-customers might make finding them sound like a challenge. But with the right tools and some know-how, tracking down customers in cyber-space is a snap.

Tracking down e-customers

The Internet provides you with a wealth of ways to find your customers, business leads, and business opportunities. Start in the following virtual places:

✔ **B2B (Business to Business) exchanges:** A source of great e-trade leads, these exchanges often specialize in sectors like metals, apparel, and forest products. They provide a more secure e-business environment than what you find in the online international marketplace. Check with your domestic industry association, or try some of the following links to start:

- Electronic Commerce Europe: (www.eceurope.com) A directory of over 430,000 international companies and government organizations around the world

- Federation of International Trade Associations: (www.fita.org/tradehub.html) Includes a buy/sell exchange and world trade leads

- Foreign Trade On-line: (www.foreign-trade.com) A B2B portal with foreign trade information for exporters and importers

- Import Export Business Center: (www.importexporthelp.com) Offers B2B exchanges, as well as online marketing tools

- WorldtradeAA.com: (www.worldtradeaa.com) An international B2B directory of exporters and importers

✔ **International marketplaces:** (www.sourcecan.com) Through the SourceCAN.com Opportunity Matching service, you can receive sales opportunities that are specific to your business. You can even filter which leads you get, so set it as broadly or as narrowly as you prefer. SourceCAN also helps you find business partners and lets you post jobs (such as contracts for shipping services you require that other companies can bid on) that you want to outsource.

✔ **Online advertising:** Research Web sites that relate to your product or service and enquire about putting a banner ad or a link to your own business Web site. Just be sure those sites are reputable. You don't want your business's name associated with anything that has a less-than-stellar reputation.

✔ **Search engines:** (AltaVista, Google, MSN, and Yahoo, for example.) These help Internet users find Web sites on specific topics. So, in addition to researching and seeking out customers, make it easy for customers to find you. Get your business's Web site listed with major international search engines. Ask your Web developer or Web hosting service to do this for you.

✔ **Virtual Trade Commissioner:** (infoexport.gc.ca) Your Virtual Trade Commissioner can provide you with international business leads from trade commissioners abroad.

Investigating potential e-customers

After you've used the Internet to track down a few potential customers who seem promising, don't just plunge into e-business with them head-first. Just like in traditional exporting businesses, do what you can to ensure that your customers are trustworthy and will be worth doing business with. In fact, you may even feel the need to be extra vigilant, because you may not have had any face-to-face contact with these virtual customers. Keep these ideas in mind before you make a commitment to a new customer:

✔ **Who is the potential customer?** Check the customer's address to be sure it actually exists. Don't go ahead with the deal if the customer is too unavailable or unwilling to provide basic information — these signs could point to fraud.

✔ **Does the potential customer have solid credit?** Assessing credit is important. Be aware that incidents of online credit card fraud are on the rise in some areas of the world, so be wary of accepting credit card payments from these markets.

✔ **How much do you know about the potential customer's country?** Due diligence is key. Speak to fellow exporters or check with your trade association to find out about others' experiences with your target market. Think twice about doing business in a country that has an untrustworthy business reputation. If you hear a lot of stories of fraud or kickbacks, for example, in a certain country, leads to that country may not be worth following.

E-customer support

You have some good ideas for how to get customers to buy from you. But how do you get them to keep coming back? You know the importance of providing excellent customer support. In fact, that may be one of the ways you developed your business in Canada and made it competitive and successful.

The first step for providing great electronic customer support is to make sure your company's e-mail address is prominently featured on your Web site. Then, check the e-mail regularly and respond to any customer inquiries as soon as possible.

Because technology has come such a long way in recent years, sometimes traditional methods of customer support (fax, phone, mail) just don't cut it. For your e-business, consider looking into *electronic customer relations management* (eCRM) — communicating with your customers and satisfying their needs electronically. You can communicate with your customers more efficiently, keep them happy, and get that competitive edge your exporting business needs to succeed. You can purchase eCRM systems, which run over the Internet as Web applications, or arrange for eCRM services through your Application Service Provider (ASP).

E-customer privacy

Protecting your customers' privacy must be a priority for you; after all, it sure is for your customers. Besides, laws are in place regarding how Canadian businesses collect, use, or disclose personal information about customers obtained during business transactions.

Since January 1, 2004, your business has had to abide by Canada's Personal Information Protection and Electronic Documents Act (PIPEDA). PIPEDA laws don't just apply in Canada. They also apply to international commercial transactions during which personal information is exchanged. To get more information about issues of privacy and how they affect your exporting e-business, visit the Office of the Privacy Commissioner of Canada at www.privcom.gc.ca.

Getting Paid if You're an E-Business

Your e-business can receive payment from international customers through the methods we explain in Chapter 5. But, if you're a retail business, customers often pay by credit card.

If taking credit card payments directly isn't possible or you're not comfortable with this type of payment (refer to "Investigating e-customers," earlier in this chapter), you have the option of hiring a specialized online company. The company collects your customers' payments, which can be credit card payments or bank transfers, and then gives them to you (and charges a transaction fee, of course). PayPal is an example of this type of company.

Internet transactions aren't always 100 percent secure. But online companies that collect your international payments usually offer security features that you may not have if you take payments yourself. These companies safeguard your and your customers' private information and may offer fraud-detection services and protect you against customer *charge-backs* (a credit card transaction that gets billed back to you, after the sale has taken place).

E-business resources

If you want to look more deeply into e-business and how it benefits your exporting venture, the following resources can help you out.

✔ **Business Development Bank of Canada:** The BDC has lots of information for Canadian e-business owners, and even offers financing and consulting services (www.bdc.ca).

✔ **CanadaBusiness.gc.ca:** The Government of Canada Web portal links you to loads of e-business resources (canadabusiness.gc.ca).

✔ **Canadian e-Business Initiative:** This public–private sector partnership is an informational Web site that aims to help Canada's e-businesses succeed, with a focus on productivity, leadership, and innovation (www.cebi.ca).

Part III
Meeting Standards and Keeping It Legal

The 5th Wave   By Rich Tennant

GRICHTENNANT

"Sorry Mr. and Mrs. Binney. Law school didn't prepare me for this kind of contract negotiation."

In this part...

In any business, but particularly in the exporting business, all kinds of rules and regulations exist, and they can get pretty complicated.

This part gets into all that legalese you face with standards and contracts, and tells you what to keep in mind when doing business internationally. It also tells you about intellectual property laws and how to protect your rights.

Chapter 9

Legal Stuff: International Standards and Contracts

● ●

In This Chapter

▶ Knowing about international standards

▶ Checking out international contracts

▶ Giving proper law its props

▶ Looking at contracts for selling goods

▶ Investigating contracts for selling services

● ●

*J*ust when you've wrapped your head around all the laws, standards, and contracts that matter to you and your domestic business, you decide to enter into the international marketplace. Congratulations — you get to put your mind to work and learn a whole new set of rules and regulations.

Although you can — in fact, doing so is a good idea — hire a professional who specializes in the legalities of international trade, having a decent understanding of the rules is always helpful. Get to know the ins and outs of your foreign target market's standards and contracts. The more you know, the more capable you are of running your business and making day-to-day decisions in that market. Then, use the lawyer to take care of the details.

This chapter looks at the concept of international standards, what to keep in mind when working with international contracts, and special circumstances for contracts for goods and contracts for services.

Meeting International Standards

Standards certainly aren't a new concept to you. Because consumers rely on standards established by outside bodies to ensure their safety, it's your job to adhere to them. They vary widely depending on context, depending on what it is you're exporting. According to product (good or service), and according to the criteria for imports a country's governing body establishes. To export to any given country you need to become familiar with their regulatory standards.

As an exporter, you want to ensure that your product or service meets the regulatory standards of your new target market. If not, you must upgrade or adjust your product or service accordingly.

Adopting international standards for your exporting business has three major benefits:

- ✔ **You're more competitive:** The more you comply with existing standards, the faster and easier you get into foreign markets.

- ✔ **You save money:** Adopting international standards means that you can avoid the cost and complications — testing and recertification, for instance — associated with moving into new markets.

- ✔ **You improve communications:** Complying with international standards makes the exchange of technical information with experts in other countries easier.

Finding out more about standards

The standards of each market in each country are obviously too extensive to list in this book, as are the total number of standards organizations. But you can begin your research in a few key places. Check out the Standards Council of Canada (SCC) at www.scc.ca. This is an extensive site that links you to many more sites that may help you locate your exact product and market, so be sure to investigate thoroughly.

Although each industry is controlled by its own standards board, you can investigate two chief international standards forums right away:

✔ **The International Organization for Standardization (ISO):** The ISO develops the largest number of standards in the world. The ISO's main focus is on developing technical standards for engineers and manufacturers. Check them out at www.iso.org.

✔ **The International Electrotechnical Commission (IEC):** The IEC creates standards for anything related to electrics or electronics. These standards are the basis for international contracts in this field. Check them out at www.iec.ch.

Looking at Standards Council of Canada programs

Because standards are constantly evolving, staying on top of them is difficult. The Standards Council of Canada (SCC) can help by doing the legwork for you. They offer three programs that can help keep you on top of international standards:

✔ **Export Alert!:** This program provides e-mail notifications of proposals in the global market for regulatory changes.

✔ **RegWatch:** This is a database that contains all standards references in federal legislation.

✔ **Standards Alert!:** Through this program you can keep an eye on Canadian, International Standard for Organization (ISO), and Electrotechnical Commission (IEC) standards (we talk about the ISO and IEC programs earlier in this chapter). You can be notified automatically of changes, which means you have one less thing to worry about during your busy day.

For more information on these programs, visit the SCC Web site (www.scc.ca). Go to the "for industry" section and follow the links to "SCC programs and services."

Determining HS codes

If you plan to export a product or good, you must be aware of the *Harmonized Commodity Description and Coding System*, or HS system for short. HS codes belong to an international system that classifies traded goods into six-digit categories, depending on what they are. For example, vegetables and fruits are in one category; machinery and mechanical devices are in another.

The World Customs Organization developed and maintains the HS codes (www.wcoomd.org). About 200 countries (which is most countries in the world) use the HS system to determine duties on traded goods, to collect data, and to standardize international trade systems.

The Canada Border Services Agency (www.cbsa-asfc.gc.ca) and the border agencies of other countries require you to report your exports' HS codes so that they can collect export-related statistics, control the exporting of dangerous goods or regulated goods, and control how goods move across various borders through different countries.

You need to determine what HS codes apply to the products you're exporting. You report the code to a designated export reporting office in your target market so that the border services organization of that country can track products and create statistics. Statistics Canada can help you determine relevant HS codes (www.statcan.ca/english/tradedata/cec/index.htm), and you can visit the Canada Border Services Agency Web site for more information.

Using International Contracts

A *contract* is an agreement between two parties. Seems pretty simple and just like something you're already doing. The difference is that, when you're talking about international contracts, things become a bit more complicated.

Differing business and legal regimes are big technical hurdles to overcome in forming a contract. The fact is, however, you're not a lawyer, you're a businessperson. The difficulties that you personally deal with in business contracts may stem more from things like language barriers, cultural differences, and geography. At the end of the day, you rely on your lawyer to fine-tune all of the details for you. But negotiations are a lot easier if you speak the same language — both literally and figuratively — as the party with whom you're making an agreement.

A few different issues can cause contractual misunderstandings in international business. Here are a few to watch out for:

✔ **Different legal regimes:** Perhaps in your target market, it's legal for the buyer to terminate a contract without notice within fifteen days of signing. But in your domestic market, after you sign on the dotted line you're in it for the long haul. If you aren't aware of these kinds of legal issues, you might find yourself disputing a contract that is actually perfectly legal in the foreign market.

✔ **Different business standards:** In a specific industry in a foreign market, it may be standard for a contract to state that the seller is responsible for all warranties and guarantees, even after the sale is over. But in your experience, they are the buyer's responsibility after the goods are sold. Be sure you're aware of the contract laws in your foreign market so nothing comes as a surprise.

✔ **Not fully understanding the contract's terms:** This kind of misunderstanding could result from a language barrier or just not bothering to read the contract thoroughly. Always get your lawyer, intermediary — whoever is helping you to read the contracts — to make sure you don't miss anything.

Above all, when you're dealing with contracts, always read through them carefully. Never, ever assume that something is included or understood unless you've read it in black and white — especially if you're not totally familiar with the way things go in your target market. After all, you've heard what assuming things makes you out to be, don't you?

✔ **Poorly drawn-up contracts:** Don't trust a customer who claims they'll handle the contract and all you have to do is sign. An incomplete contract can leave holes a mile wide that the buyer can jump through later on.

A misinterpreted word or cultural gesture can have a serious effect on a business transaction (see Chapter 2). The more aware you are of these differences, the easier conducting hassle-free transactions will be. Avoiding these obstacles is even more critical when negotiating contracts; you don't want a simple misunderstanding to become a deal-breaker.

Because you and your foreign customer are likely accustomed to very different business practices, ensure that your contract is precise, specific, and all-encompassing. Avoiding disputes in business whenever possible is always the best practice. To avoid a dispute, make sure that both parties have a mutual understanding of the terms of the contract. A contract that's specific and clear is important to avoiding a legal battle.

Defining Proper Law

Simply put, *proper law* refers to the laws that are binding in the country in which you're doing business. Consequently, you may deal with different proper law in each country you do business. Many issues arise in international contracts because of the different definitions of a contract itself. In some countries, a verbal contract is binding. In others, you must put all your terms in writing. In some countries, laws state that persons who are not a party to a contract have certain rights, but in other countries, they have none.

Be sure to familiarize yourself with the laws of each country in which you're doing business so that your contracts are always written in terms of proper law.

Looking at Contracts for Selling Goods

You're selling something that the buyer is buying. As soon as you give the buyer your good and he gives you the set amount of money for that good, a sale has taken place. The contract that covers that sale outlines the agreement that made that entire transaction happen — hopefully, in as smooth a manner as possible.

Goods are material things (including real estate) that you are selling. If what you're selling is intangible, such as patents or services (see "Looking at Contracts for Selling Service," later in this Chapter), it's not considered a good. Of course, we're sure that your service is *good*, but it's not *a* good.

Because selling goods involves the exchange of money, transactions during which no money changes hands, such as barter or counter-trade, are in a different category.

Your contract for selling goods needs to stipulate many conditions to keep the transaction on track. Be sure that the contract covers the following elements:

✔ The goods that you're selling and their specifications (e.g., materials from which they're made, their size and weight)

✔ The amount or number of goods that you're selling

✔ The total price of the goods, and perhaps the cost-per-unit (the price of each individual good) and any discount or special rate you're giving the buyer

✔ Any international standards to which the goods must conform (we discuss standards earlier in this chapter)

✔ The date you're shipping the goods and the goods' port of entry (the geographical location where they enter the importing country)

✔ The date (or approximate date) that the goods will arrive at their destination

✔ The *carrier* (the person or company that transports the goods from one place to another)

✔ Any other conditions that relate to the goods' delivery (if they'll be shipped by plane, if they'll be delivered to a warehouse or office, etc.)

When you write the terms of delivery on your contract, knowing common International Commerce (INCO) terms is helpful. The International Chamber of Commerce created a common vocabulary for international trade. Check out www.iccwbo.org/index_incoterms.asp for more information.

✔ Any insurance you have on the goods and what it covers (loss or damage, and up to what amount)

✔ The circumstances (if any) under which the buyer can reject the goods after you've shipped them

✔ The way the buyer is paying you, such as letter of credit or payment in advance (we discuss these methods in Chapter 5)

✔ The details of any return policy in case the buyer is not satisfied after the purchase, and any warranties or guarantees on the goods

✔ The measures that you can take if either you or the buyer violates any of the contract's terms

Looking at Contracts for Selling Services

Contracts for selling services are different from those for selling goods. Because no actual transfer of product takes place in the sale of services, "methods of delivery" can vary, and legal contracts can range from a one-line description to pages and pages of technical specifications.

Both parties must understand a few important issues, regardless of the agreed upon form of delivery. The contract should answer the following questions:

- What service are you providing, and who is providing it?
- When do you start providing service and when do you stop? Do you do so on specific dates, or does it depend on when the work is finished?
- When and how much will you get paid?
- Can you or your customer terminate the contract, and under what circumstances can you do so?
- What happens if the contract is terminated? Do you hand over the work completed to date? Could either party pay a penalty fee?
- Do you need to follow any rules of confidentiality?
- Do you need any special insurance to perform the service in your target market, and can you get this insurance?
- What happens if your customer can't provide information or facilities for your business to perform the services that were agreed upon in the original contract?
- Can your customer refuse to pay you under certain conditions? If so, what are those conditions?
- What are the procedures for resolving disputes that may arise during the delivery of your service?
- Can the customer renew or extend the contract?

Chapter 10

Protecting Your Intellectual Property

· ·

In This Chapter

▶ Smartening up about intellectual property

▶ Understanding patents

▶ Getting copyrights right

▶ Finding out about trademarks

▶ Investigating industrial designs

▶ Figuring out integrated circuit typography

· ·

*I*f you're a cautious sort, you might write your name into a book before you loan it to someone. You can't do that with an idea. If you don't have firm evidence that an idea is yours, you could be out a lot of money and spend a lot of time in court. Protecting your intellectual property is an important part of exporting.

This chapter looks at why protecting your creation is important, the different types of intellectual property that exist, and how you can protect what's rightfully yours, even in a foreign market.

Defining Intellectual Property

Intellectual property (as opposed to physical property) refers to the intangible or intellectual nature of something that arises from human creativity.

Here's an example: Think of an ordinary household item, such as a toaster. That toaster has both physical and intellectual properties. The physical property component is the toaster itself, as an object. The intellectual property components are all the materials that went into creating the toaster, like preliminary drawings and plans for how its heating device would work.

Intellectual property law protects all kinds of things, such as

- ✔ New inventions
- ✔ Designs
- ✔ Writings
- ✔ Films

You may have an intellectual property in what you export, and you have a right to that intellectual property. But what exactly are *intellectual property rights*? Well, they protect your right, as the creator of an idea, to exclude others from using that idea without your consent. After all, that idea's yours, darn it!

Investigate the intellectual property laws of your intended market before you pursue business there. Some countries will not uphold your trademark, for example, and taking legal action to fix the situation can be difficult and costly. Always check with the Canadian Intellectual Property Office or a patent agent or lawyer to know how you can protect your creations.

Intellectual property comes in five main forms, which we explain in the upcoming sections of this chapter.

Patents

A *patent* is a document that the Canadian government issues that describes your creation. It applies to the physical invention itself or to the process you used to make it a material object. An abstract idea or principle (like the great idea you have for a water-purifying system) doesn't qualify for a patent.

To qualify for a patent, your creation must be

- ✔ New
- ✔ Useful
- ✔ Inventive (meaning not just anyone could have created it)

You apply to the Canadian Intellectual Property Office (CIPO) (www.cipo.gc.ca) to obtain a patent. The application must include a drawing of your invention, an abstract, a petition, and a filing fee. The filing fees vary depending on the intricacy of your invention, but expect to pay at least $2,000 to $3,000 or more. Visit CIPO's Web site for the online application tutorial, step-by-step description of the process, and fees.

Patent laws are national, so if you're exporting a good that you've patented in Canada, that patent doesn't apply in other countries. You have to apply for a separate patent in your target market.

In Canada and the U.S., you don't have to file for your patent right away when you create your invention. You can wait to file for up to one year after the time you've made the invention public (you generally don't want to wait that long, though). However, most foreign countries don't provide the grace period. Be sure to apply for patent protection in your target market *before* you've gone public with your invention there. If you go public with your unpatented invention in some countries, you can't stop other manufacturers from copying it.

Here are a few links to international patent offices to get you started:

- United States Patent and Trademark Office (USPTO): patents.uspto.gov/

- World Intellectual Property Organization (WIPO): www.wipo.int/portal/index.html.en

- Espacenet, a network of European patent databases: www.espacenet.com

- Japan Patent Office: www.jpo.go.jp

A *patent agent* or *patent lawyer* is a professional who knows the ins and outs of applying for a patent. Consider hiring a patent agent particularly when you apply for a patent in a foreign country. The process can be tricky, and a patent agent has the expertise to help you.

Copyrights

Copyright is the exclusive right of the creator or copyright holder to sell or publish certain types of work (just think of "right to copy"). Copyright applies for these kinds of works:

- ✔ Literary works — novels, poems, or short stories
- ✔ Dramatic works — plays
- ✔ Musical works — songs (but not their lyrics, those are considered literary works)
- ✔ Artistic works — paintings
- ✔ Performed works — dances
- ✔ Communication signals — radio signals
- ✔ Sound recordings — a recorded radio show, for instance

After you create a work that falls into one of these categories (you choreograph a dance show that you're planning to stage in countries overseas, for example), copyright is automatic and you don't have to apply for it.

If you're concerned that you may have to prove you own the copyright to your creation someday, try this: mail documents to yourself that describe the copyright item (sheet music, script for your play). Don't open the documents when you receive them. The postmark proves that the idea was yours on a specific date.

If you live in Canada, you almost always get automatic copyright protection. The Canadian copyright also applies in foreign countries that have signed the Berne, Universal Copyright, or Rome conventions, or the WTO agreement, which the great majority of foreign countries have done. But check with your lawyer to be sure your that copyright applies in your target market.

To take your copyright a step further and get it registered, apply to the Copyright Office of CIPO (`www.cipo.gc.ca`). Their Web site also has links to international intellectual property sites.

Trademarks

A *trademark* is a word, design, or a combination of both, that distinguishes your goods or services from the goods or services of others. It's a personal stamp, if you will. Take, for example, the *For Dummies* on the cover of this book. It's a trademark, which prevents anyone other than Wiley, the publisher, from producing *For Dummies* materials.

File an application for a trademark with CIPO's Trademarks Office. You can apply online (www.cipo.gc.ca) in the "Trademarks" section) or print out an application and mail it in. If you register your trademark, you have exclusive rights to use it in Canada. You can renew that right for fifteen-year periods.

Registering your trademark in Canada doesn't protect your trademark in other countries. To register in your target market, contact a *trademark agent*, a professional who creates your application and knows the ins and outs of the trademark system (find a list of agents at www.cipo.gc.ca, in the "Trade-marks" section). You can also contact the Canadian embassy in your target market to know more about their trademark registration procedures. Check out Foreign Affairs and International Trade Canada's Web site at www.international.gc.ca to find the relevant embassy.

New businesses should always make sure that no other businesses have registered the trademark or tradename they plan to use. A trademark agent can determine this for you, or you can search the Trade-marks Database on CIPO's Web site.

Industrial Designs

An industrial design is the shape, pattern, or ornamentation (or a combination of these elements) that applies to a manufactured product. It doesn't apply to the product's utilitarian features, just its aesthetic ones. The unique pattern embroidered on the cowboy boots you export, for example, is an industrial design.

You can register your industrial design with CIPO. Include the application form, a drawing or photograph of the design, and the application fee. See CIPO's Web site for detailed information.

You have to register your industrial design in your target market. Canadian registration doesn't apply outside this country. Hire a patent agent (find an agent through CIPO's Web site) to help you register in foreign countries and consult the Canadian embassy in your target market.

Integrated Circuit Typography

Yup, that's quite a mouthful for something that's really very small. In essence, *integrated circuit typography* (ITC) is the circuitry used in microchips and semiconductor chips. You can find them in electronic devices like DVD players and MP3 players, for example.

To register your ICT, submit an application form (available on CIPO's Web site at (www.cipo.gc.ca) and a $200 fee to the Registrar of Integrated Circuit Typography.

Like most other forms of intellectual property that we discuss in this chapter, ICT protection in Canada doesn't apply internationally. Hire an agent to help you register your ICT in foreign countries, or consult the Canadian embassy in your target market.

Part IV
The Part of Tens

The 5th Wave   By Rich Tennant

"How many times have I told you that you can't export your brother? You don't have any of the proper documentation, and that packing is completely inadequate."

In this part...

*Y*ou know where you want to go and how to get your product or service there, but where can you turn for a little bit of help? No problem.

This part is made up of easy-to-understand lists. One tells you about a few important resources that can give you a leg up. The other outlines the ten big steps of exporting, from planning all the way to closing the deal.

Chapter 11

Ten (Okay, Six) Resources to Help You

● ●

In This Chapter

▶ Checking out organizations to help you with your exporting venture

● ●

*S*till think you're all alone as a Canadian exporter? No way. Lots of organizations want to help your exporting business succeed and give you many tools to make it happen.

Agriculture and Agri-Food Canada

Agriculture and Agri-Food Canada helps Canadian agricultural sector businesses to compete with world markets.

Agriculture and Agri-Food Canada offer the Agri-Food Trade Service Web site. The trade service is a central portal of export information for Canadian businesses in the agricultural and fish and seafood industries. This site takes you from your initial inquiry right through to your target market. Through the site, you can access market information, trade counselling, and export support activities. Visit Agriculture and Agri-Food Canada at ats.agr.gc.ca.

Canada Mortgage and Housing Corporation

CMHC International helps exporters' businesses grow internationally by helping them identify new housing and export opportunities in potential markets. CMHC gives your export business promotional support, organizes trade missions, provides matchmaking services, and promotes Canadian business acumen overseas.

Go to the CMHC Web site at www.cmhc.ca/international to find information on the following topics, and more:

✔ **Taking Your Business Abroad:** Information about export opportunities for the Canadian housing industry

✔ **International Housing News:** An e-newsletter

✔ **International Markets:** Housing export strategies and export opportunities

✔ **International Regulations:** Answers to frequently asked questions on international codes and standards

The CMHC International Web site also offers inspirational success stories to get you motivated.

Canadian Heritage

The federal government's Trade Routes sector program is a helpful trade development program designed specifically for small- to medium-sized businesses in arts and culture. It provides cultural sector entrepreneurs with international business development opportunities. Go to www.canadianheritage.gc.ca/routes for more information.

Canadian Intellectual Property Office (CIPO)

Protecting your intellectual property at home and abroad is in your business's best interests, as we discuss in Chapter 10.

Visit the CIPO Web site (www.cipo.gc.ca) for complete information about forms of intellectual property, patents and trademarks databases, and details of applications and registration fees. CIPO also provides links to international intellectual property associations.

Foreign Affairs and International Trade Canada

This government department gives Canadian business the information and support they need to succeed in the international marketplace. Research trade agreements and negotiations that may affect your export venture and get information about travelling overseas and passports.

Foreign Affairs and International Trade Canada also has multiple resources specifically for Canadian exporters such as:

- ✔ ExportSource, a Web site dedicated to helping new exporters crack new markets, with helpful step-by-step guides and advice on trading with the United States (exportsource.ca)
- ✔ InfoExport, which is the Canadian Trade Commissioner Service that provides contacts and expert advice (infoexport.gc.ca)

Trade Team Canada Sectors

You get the benefit of teamwork by using resources from Trade Team Canada Sectors (TTCSs). TTCSs are partnerships between federal and provincial governments, firms, and industry associations. They have shared priorities and combine resources to promote Canadian products and services. TTCSs cover the following sectors:

- ✔ Aerospace and defence
- ✔ Agriculture, food, and beverages
- ✔ Automotive
- ✔ Bio-industries

- ✔ Bio-Industries
- ✔ Building products
- ✔ Cultural goods and services
- ✔ Electric power equipment and services
- ✔ Environmental industries
- ✔ Health industries
- ✔ Information and communications technologies
- ✔ Oil and gas equipment and services
- ✔ Plastics
- ✔ Services industries

Visit `ttcs.ic.gc.ca` and click the link that best describes your industry.

Chapter 12

Ten (Okay, Nine) Steps of Exporting

● ●

In This Chapter

▶ Looking at the steps to follow in your exporting venture

● ●

*T*his chapter shows you how the whole process plays out and warns you of any obstacles you might encounter along the way. Of course, every exporter's experience is different, but our little summary gives you a general idea of what to expect when you're exporting.

Deciding If You Want to Export

If you read Part I of this book, you know that this stage is crucial. Without a solid roadmap to guide you, how will your goods find their way to your target market? Here are the first two steps to successful planning:

1. Assess your business's potential as an exporter (Chapter 1).

2. Think about the pros and cons of getting into the exporting business (Chapter 1).

Performing Market Research

You've decided your business is good to export. But where will your product or service fit in best? To determine the best market for you, follow these steps:

1. Examine the types of international markets that are available for your product or service (Chapter 2).

2. Perform market research to choose the market(s) that best suit your product or service (Chapter 2). This includes collecting economic data through journals and online databases.

Ask the Canadian Trade Commissioner (Chapter 2) in your target market for special advice about the country where your target market is located.

3. Visit potential markets to gather more information about them than you would by phone or e-mail correspondence or by word-of-mouth. Face-to-face contact helps you assess their needs and how your product or service fulfills those needs (Refer to Chapter 2).

Developing Your Export Plan

You've narrowed down your target market through lots of market research and feel like you know it pretty well. The next step is to start thinking about how you're going to get your product or service there:

1. Revisit your domestic business plan and be sure it's solid (Chapter 3).

2. Create an export plan based on your domestic business plan (Chapter 3).

3. Decide on your market entry strategy for when you introduce your product to your target market (Chapter 3).

Pricing and Promoting

Exporting to a new market is no time to keep secrets. You must let everyone and their uncle know that your product or service is available and that it is fantastic. Start with these steps:

1. Think about how you will promote and advertise your product or service (Chapter 4).

2. Set a price for your good or service in your international target market. Remember that supply and demand, the competition, and your costs are all factors to consider when pricing a product (Chapter 4).

3. Create promotional packages that describe your business and its products or services, including brochures, DVDs, and business cards (refer to Chapter 4).

Getting Your Finances in Order

Your exporting business won't go very far if your finances are a mess, and it certainly won't make it across the Canadian border. Take two vital financial planning steps: Create a budget and plan out your cash flow (Chapter 5).

You may find that you're a bit short of money. Or you may feel you could take your export business even further if you had more money. Well luckily, the Government of Canada has organizations in place that offer financial services to exporters, such as Export Development Canada and the Business Development Bank of Canada (Chapter 5).

Doing the Legwork: Getting Inside Your Target Market

You've got your plan in place, so how are you going to set the wheels in motion? You have many business practices to choose from in your export business. Will you use the direct or indirect export method to get your goods into the hands of customers (Chapter 6)?

Also, you may find that no matter how you try, you can't clone yourself, and you need a bit of help. Consider hiring an intermediary to help you win over your target market (Chapter 6).

If you choose to work with an agent or distributor (Chapter 6), make a list of the best candidates, including their pros and cons. Then select the best ones for your export business.

When you know your export method and who your partners are, think about the logistics of getting your goods out there. Keep in mind international shipping rules, and documents for which you might use a freight forwarder or a customs broker (once again, Chapter 6 is good for what ails you).

Keeping Things Legal

Just like you follow regulations and laws for your domestic business, you have to do the same for your export business. You may even face a small dispute or two (Chapter 9).

Also, remember that another legal aspect is protecting what is yours — your intellectual property. Chapter 10 gets into patents, copyright, and trademarks and tells you how to protect them in a foreign market.

Sealing the Deal

Although you're an upstanding, honest person, you simply can't do business with a handshake. To make your transaction legit and to make sure you don't get ripped off, you and your customer must have a contract, which we talk about in Chapter 9.

Getting Paid

You've worked really hard to get to this point, and hopefully all the effort pays off, literally.

Your international customers aren't going to mail you cash in an envelope (and you wouldn't take the risk anyway!). You can get paid for international orders in many ways, such as letters of credit or cash in advance. Other methods, like using an open account, aren't very favourable to you, so read Chapter 5 to choose the best payment method for your business.

Appendix:

Exporting Terms

In This Appendix

▶Understanding some general exporting terms

*E*ntering a new industry sometimes means having to learn a whole new vocabulary. This appendix lays out some of the most-used international trade terms that you need to know, so you can really talk the talk (or at least understand it if you're the quiet type).

Agent: A foreign representative who sells the exporter's product in the target market.

Anti-dumping duty: An imposed duty that offsets the price impact of dumping that is materially harmful to domestic producers (see **Dumping**).

Area control list: A list of countries to which you cannot export without a permit.

Bill of lading: A contract that the carrier or freight forwarder prepares with the owner of the goods. The foreign customer needs this document to take possession of the goods.

Budget: A document or spreadsheet that outlines all of your business's planned expenses.

Carrier: The person or company that transports goods from one place to another.

Cash flow: The money that comes in and goes out of a business.

Cash in advance (Advance payment or cash up-front): A foreign customer pays a Canadian exporter before it actually receives the goods. For the exporter, this is the most secure form of payment.

Certificate of origin: A document that certifies a shipment's country of origin.

Commercial invoice: A document the exporter or freight forwarder prepares. The foreign customer requires this invoice to prove ownership and to arrange to pay the exporter.

Confirming house: A company based in a foreign country that acts as the foreign customer's agent and places orders with Canadian exporters. They also guarantee payment to the exporters.

Consignment: Delivering goods to the customer or distributor, who agrees to sell the goods and then pay the Canadian exporter. The exporter does not get paid if the goods aren't sold and retains ownership of the goods.

Consular invoice: A foreign consul issues this statement in the exporting country. It describes the goods purchased.

Contract: A legally binding agreement between two parties.

Copyright: Protection of authors or creators of literary, artistic, dramatic, and music works, and sound recordings.

Countervailing duties: When subsidized imports cause material injury to domestic industry (in the importing country), the importing country imposes duties to offset government subsidies in an exporting country.

Cross-licensing: A form of partnership where each firm licenses products or services to the other. Cross-licensing is a basic way for companies to share their products or services.

Customs broker: A company that gets goods cleared through customs, prepares customs documentation, and pays duties on exported goods for a fee.

Customs invoice: A document used to clear goods through customs in the importing country.

Direct exporting: Marketing and selling your product or service directly to the customer.

Draft (Bill of exchange): A written order for a specific amount to be paid from one party to another. A sight draft requires that the party owing pays immediately. A term draft requires that the party owing pays over a specified period of time.

Distributor: A foreign company that agrees to buy a Canadian exporter's products and is responsible for storing, marketing, and selling them (see also **Importer**).

Dumping: When an imported good or service is cheaper than similar domestically produced goods or services.

E-business: Electronic business, using Internet-based technology to conduct business such as buying and selling of products or services.

Export permit: A legal document that is required to export goods, specifically to countries on the Export Control List or countries on the area control list.

Export quotas: Limits on the amount of certain goods that can be exported at a particular time.

Export subsidies: Government payments or other benefits that domestic producers or exporters receive that are dependent on the export of their goods or services.

Exporter: A businessperson or a company that ships goods out of their home country to sell or distribute in a foreign country.

Franchise: A specific form of licensing. The franchise has the right to use a set of manufacturing or service delivery processes and established business systems and trademarks that a contractual agreement controls.

Freight forwarder: A company that handles all aspects of export shipping, for a fee.

Goods: Material, physical, moveable products that an exporter can sell and that an importer/customer can buy.

Gross domestic/national product (GDP/GNP): The total value of all of the goods and services that a country produces.

Harmonized Commodity Description and Coding System: HS system for short. HS codes are an international system that classifies traded goods into six-digit categories, depending on what they are, to keep track of exports.

Importer: A businessperson or company that brings goods from a foreign market into their home country.

Indirect exporting: Getting your product or service into your target market with the help of an intermediary.

Intellectual property: A collective term that refers to new ideas, inventions, designs, writings, films, etc., which are protected by copyright, patents, and trademarks.

Intermediary: Someone who acts for the exporter as distributor, sales representative, sales or marketing agent, or broker, or who performs similar functions.

Letter of credit: A document issued by a bank on behalf of an importer that guarantees an exporter will get paid for goods or services, providing that the terms of credit are met.

Licensing: A firm sells the rights to use its products or service, but retains some control. Licensing may lead to a partnership.

Market entry: The ways you introduce your new product or service into your target market.

NAFTA: The North American Free Trade Agreement is an agreement between Canada, the United States, and Mexico to eliminate trade barriers and encourage trade and investment between countries.

Non-tariff barriers: Government policies that distort trade, such as import quotas and discriminatory measures.

Open account: An arrangement where the Canadian exporter ships goods to a foreign customer before receiving payment. This is a risky form of payment.

Packing list: A document the exporter prepares that shows the quantity and type of goods being shipped to the foreign customer.

Patent: The right of the patent holder (within the country that granted or recognizes the patent) to prevent all others from using, making, or selling the patented subject for a specified period of time.

Proper law: The laws that are binding in the country in which you're doing business.

Services: The non-material equivalent of goods.

Standards: A formalized set of measures that businesses or government entities must follow to ensure fair and safe business practices.

Supply and demand: The amount of a particular good available and the amount of customers who want the good.

Surcharge or surtax: An extra tariff or tax on imports used as a safeguard.

Target market: The defined group of customers or geographical area to which you plan to sell your good or service.

Tariff: A tax imposed on imported goods, virtually non-existent under NAFTA since January 2003.

Trademark: A word, logo, shape or design, or type of lettering that identifies a company or a particular product.

Trading house: A company that specializes in exporting and importing the goods of other companies.